Super Omnia Bonae Voluntatis

Mission of the Maiden

A Hero Is Chosen Series
Hero Stories of the Saints

Book One

Reflections of an Uncommon Monk
Toward a Theology of Hero-Sainthood

Book Two

Mission of the Maiden
The Hero Story of Joan of Arc

Book Three

God's Good Servant and the King's
The Hero Story of Thomas More

Book Four

King of Kings
The Hero Story of Jesus of Nazareth

Book Five

Friar, Priest, and Martyr
The Hero Story of Maximilian Kolbe

Book Six

A Vocation Story Never Told
A Hero Story of Future Saints

Book Seven

Hero Bible Verses
Meditations of a Saint

Mission of the Maiden

The Hero Story of Joan of Arc

Brother Emmanuel Labrise, O.S.B.

A Hero Is Chosen

Book Two

Saint Joseph Books

Table of Contents

Introduction to the Series.. i

Introduction to Book Two... vii

Important Dates.. xiii

Part One: Historical Context

1. Charles, Dauphin of France (1428) 1

2. The Great Famine (1315 to 1322) 3

3. The Hundred Years' War (1337 to 1347) 7

4. The Black Death (1347 to 1351) 16

5. The Hundred Years' War (1355 to 1413) 22

6. The Avignon Papacy and the Western Schism...................................... 32

7. Byzantine Civil Wars and the Ottoman Invasion.................................. 39

8. The Rigors of Medieval Life 45

9. The Royal Family.. 53

10. The Hundred Years' War (1413 to 1429) 56

Part Two: Mission of the Maiden

11. Birth and Early Years (1412 to 1428) 67

12. Rise of the Maiden (1428 to 1429) 73

13. The Maiden Arrives 81

14. The Battle of Orléans 86

15. The Loire Campaign 94

16. The March to Reims and the Crowning of a King 99

17. Joan's True Vocation 103

18. Defeat at Paris 111

19. Life at Court to Capture 115

20. Imprisonment 121

21. Interrogation and Trial 125

22. Virgin, Hero, Martyr, Saint 137

23. The Hundred Years' War (1431 to 1453) 142

Conclusion 150

About the Author 159

Introduction to the Series

Reflections of an Uncommon Monk is the first book in the A Hero Is Chosen series and serves as its spiritual and moral foundation. Beginning with the second book, *Mission of the Maiden*, all of the stories build on the topics and themes introduced in *Reflections of an Uncommon Monk*. The primary aim of this series is to transmit Christian spiritual principles and to teach moral virtue in the context of a hero-saint story.

A note here should be made on the central concept and predominant themes in each book beginning with *Mission of the Maiden*. Each story, whether historical or fictional, tells the tale of one or more hero-saints called by God to a particular vocation and chosen by him to fulfill a personal mission. Historical context is crucial. A large portion of each book is dedicated to placing the protagonist within his or her historical setting in which he or she is offered an opportunity to perform a task or set of tasks, and endure an event or set of events, that qualifies him or her for hero-sainthood. In all cases except Remmy Kimm, who appears in the fiction tale, *A Vocation Story Never Told*, this occurs during the latter part of their lives, sometimes lasting years or as little as one day.

The timeframe is less important than the hero-event or hero-moment itself. One may become a hero-saint through a single heroic act at the end of one's life or through a lifetime of unselfish service. Dom Tom Mo, the other protagonist in *A Vocation Story Never Told*, was called to sacrifice his life for the passengers aboard his spacecraft within the span of a few hours. Remmy Kimm, on the other hand, was called to years of missionary service and to survive a near-death experience. Both are martyrs, one red (blood, death) and the other white (selfless service to others).

Also less important than the hero-event and hero-moment is the station in life one occupies when he or she is called. Joan of Arc was called out of obscurity to a public mission lasting less than a year and culminated in her being burned at the stake as a heretic. Thomas More was called out of prominence to sacrifice his high standing in English society and even his life for loyalty to the faith he had professed. Jesus of Nazareth was also called out of obscurity to a public ministry lasting about three years and ending with his crucifixion. The hero-event and hero-moment also eclipse whatever competencies or assets one possesses when called. With the possible exception of Saint Thomas More, all are underdog stories.

A second note should be made on where these books fit within the realm of literature. In my opinion, none of the books in this series, whether historical or fictional, is in the strict sense a work of biography, history, or fiction, even if they contain biographical accounts, historical content, or fiction. Much less are they hagiographies, even if they deal with the lives of canonized saints. They are instead hero-saint stories existing within the genre of nonfiction Christian literature.

Those who appreciate the work of Joseph Campbell, especially his highly influential *The Hero with a Thousand Faces*, might find something worthwhile in the pages of these books. I have not attempted to model the fictional characters on his writing, however, nor have I attempted to frame the retelling of these stories of actual historical persons based on his work on myth and mythical figures. It is more that I am attracted to the archetype and archetypical behavior of the hero-saint that lies deep within the unconscious of every human person, at least if you subscribe to Jungian theory. This archetype, like so many others, manifests itself in movies, books, art, and public performances of every age from antiquity to the popular films of today. It is the archetype of the hero-saint that serves as the psychological foundation for the stories in this series.

I thought it helpful to provide a brief lexicon of terms on which the reader may focus. I cannot provide definitions for each, however, as there is a certain fluidity of meaning depending on a person's life, but at least the mention of them will help to make the reader aware of the important aspects of each story and the subject matter and flavor of this series. The lexicon appears on the following page.

A Lexicon of Terms

1. Capstone experience
2. Death-leading-unto-eternity
3. Desert experience
4. Deus ex machina
5. Fulfillment in life
6. Hero quest
7. Hero story
8. Hero-adventure
9. Hero-event
10. Hero-moment
11. Hero-saint
12. Life journey
13. Meaning in life
14. Mission
15. Mission sequence
16. Mystery
17. Oceans of eternity
18. Personal holiness
19. Pilgrim
20. Pilgrimage
21. Purification
22. Purpose in life
23. Reward
24. Sainthood
25. Saint-in-the-making
26. Sanctification
27. Sands of time
28. Satisfaction in life
29. Tides of history
30. Value in life
31. Vocation
32. Wayfarer
33. Winds of change

Book Two

Mission of the Maiden

Introduction to Book Two

This humble, little book is yet another in the long line of books written about Joan of Arc. It does not aspire to add anything new to what is already in the literature, but it will offer a short, readable version of her life in its historical context, as well as a hero story in the context of the series A Hero Is Chosen.

Mission of the Maiden is about a hero-saint we know in English as "Joan of Arc," but she will not be referred to by that name past this introduction. At her trial, she is recorded to have said she was called "Jehanette" ("Little Jehanne"[1]) by the people of her home village of Domrémy, but once she left home and traveled to other parts of France to fulfill her mission, she was called "Jehanne." Although Joan testified at her trial that her father was called "Jacques d'Arc," we have no evidence that she was ever referred to as "Jehanne d'Arc" ("Joan of Arc"). On the contrary, we have contemporary accounts that testify that she often referred to herself in speech, and was known by the people of France during her public mission, as "Jehanne la Pucelle" ("Joan the Maiden,

---

[1] Pronounced *zjohn* or *zje-hahn.*

Virgin"). In addition, although she was illiterate, she learned to write her name, and we have extant letters dictated by her and signed in her own hand as "Jehanne la Pucelle."

In English, "la Pucelle" is often translated as "the Maid." The word "maid" is a shortened version of "maiden" or "maidservant." Because it is commonly used to denote a "woman employed to do housework and to clean up after others," I have chosen to translate "pucelle" as "maiden," which does not carry the connotation in English of a "female servant who does housekeeping" or "maidservant." This is important because correctly understanding "la Pucelle" in the way she and her contemporaries understood the term is key to understanding her self-image, personal identity, and how she was known in her age—which was as a "young woman and unmarried virgin." It is true she testified at her trial that she did housework when she lived at home with her parents, but there is no evidence she ever engaged in domestic service once she left Domrémy and embarked upon her mission, and it was only then that she adopted the title "la Pucelle." It was as if she were leaving one identity behind (the peasant girl her parents raised to do domestic work and other chores typical of medieval village life) and embracing another (the young virgin who responds to God's call and becomes a soldier and captain to fight for the rightful King of France and expel the unjust English invaders). Along with this mission came a new identity, a new role, and a new title—"la Pucelle."

Judging by the testimony of the witnesses who knew her at Domrémy and participated in her rehabilitation trial, the qualities she exhibited as a soldier and warrior were not evident when she was a peasant girl. Some kind of transformation seems to have taken place, as when Abram departed from Harran at God's behest and was given a new mission (to become the Father of a great nation) and a new name ("Abraham") that corresponded with a new identity. The bestowal of a new name to accompany a new mission and identity is common in Scripture (e.g., "Jacob" to "Israel," "Simon" to "Peter," "Saul" to "Paul"). When "Jehanette" departed from Domrémy, she became "Jehanne la Pucelle" ("Joan the Maiden, Virgin"), and she was never again occupied with housework or the domestic chores of her former way of life.

In English, the name "Joan" does not differentiate between "Jehanette the peasant girl and village dweller" and "Jehanne the soldier-hero-warrior," but is used to designate her identity both *before* and *after* her departure from Domrémy. It seems appropriate, however, for the reasons given above and especially with reference to this series, that some distinction should be made, and since the diminutive form of "Joan" ("Joanette") is seldom used in English, this distinction should be reflected in her title. Therefore, in this retelling of her story, I will refer to her once she embarked upon her public mission as "Joan the Maiden" rather than "Joan the Maid."

This is fitting for another reason: Joan is a famous historical figure and most people can tell you a little about her life (i.e., she was a French peasant girl who became a knight; she wore armor and carried a sword and banner; she was burned at the stake for helping the King of France against the English, etc). This was about the extent of my knowledge of her prior to researching and writing this book, but over the past year I have come to a deep respect for Joan that has blossomed into veneration.

She was by no means perfect, but she was only nineteen when she was martyred, and during her short life she demonstrated admiral character and determination that would be difficult if not impossible for most of us to emulate. I have become deeply impressed with her integrity and heroism, and my hope is that the reader will come to this same appreciation if it is not already there. A transformation has taken place in me from the "Joan as I formerly knew her" to the "Joan as I know her now"—a transformation that mirrors the one that took place in her during her earthly life from "Joan before her vocation and mission" to "Joan the hero-saint who answered God's call."

Transformations can be experienced in a particular moment in time, but they are more often than not a process that unfolds over time, and in some way, a journey. I hope you approach this book as a journey of spiritual growth that mirrors Joan's journey toward God and eternity, and as with my other books, I hope you make use of the final few pages reserved for notes and personal reflections. Most of all, I hope both of these transformations—(1) in our understanding and appreciation of Joan, and (2) in the growth in holiness that comes from answering the call to sainthood—take place in each of you.

~

One final note: I remind the reader that this book is not a biography strictly speaking, but a biographical account based on a modest amount of research that is meant to follow *Reflections of an Uncommon Monk* and incorporate some of the earlier book's ideas and concepts. *Mission of the Maiden* is the second book in a series, all of which build on *Reflections of an Uncommon Monk*, all of them stories of men and women in whose lives are demonstrated the essential aspects of heroism and Christian sainthood. The primary purpose of *Mission of the Maiden* is to give a biographical account of Joan's life in its historical context and to tell her story in the context of this series.

Important Dates
1302 to 1920

1302   Pope Boniface issues *Unam Sanctum*
       Battle of Bapheus

1303   Battle of Courtrai

1309   Beginning of the Avignon Papacy (1309–1377)

1312   Council of Vienne (1312–1314)

1322   Charles IV, King of France (r. 1322–1328)

1328   Philip VI of Valois, King of France (r. 1328–1350)
       Elected in preference to Edward III of England

1329   Edward III does homage to Philip VI for Aquitaine

1335   First papal palace built at Avignon

1337   Beginning of the Hundred Years' War

1338   Ottoman Turks reach the Bosporus

1340   Battle of Sluys

1346   Battle of Crécy
       English take Calais

1347   First outbreak in Europe of the bubonic plague

1350   John II, King of France (r. 1350–1364)

1356   Battle of Poitiers
        John II captured and taken to London

1358   Jacquerie revolt in France

1360   Treaty of Brétigny

1364   Charles V, King of France (r. 1364–1380)

1378   Beginning of the Western Schism (1378–1417)

1380   Charles VI, King of France (r. 1380–1422)

1381   English Peasants' Revolt

1384   Death of John Wycliffe

1392   Charles VI experiences first bouts of madness

1396   Dukes of Burgundy and Orléans contend for power

1403   Birth of Charles the dauphin

1407   Assassination of Louis, Duke of Orléans
        Beginning of the French civil war (1407–1435)

1410   John Hus excommunicated

1412   Birth of Joan the Maiden

1413   Henry V, King of England (r. 1413–1422)

1414   Council of Constance (1414–1417) ends Western Schism

1415   Battle of Agincourt
        Execution of John Hus

1419   Beginning of the Hussite Wars (1419–1436)

1416   John the Fearless, Duke of Burgundy, recognizes
        Henry V as King of France

1418   Burgundians capture Paris

1419   Assassination of John the Fearless, Duke of Burgundy

1420   May: Treaty of Troyes
        August: Death of Henry V of England
        October: Death of Charles VI of France
        Henry VI, King of England (r. 1422–1461, 1470–1471)
        Charles VII, King of France (r. 1422–1461)

1424   Battle of Verneuil

1428   Siege of Orléans
        Joan travels to Vaucouleurs

1429   February: Joan travels to Chinon
        May: Siege of Orléans lifted
        June: Battle of Patay
        July: Coronation of Charles VII
        September: French siege of Paris fails

1430   May: Burgundians capture Joan at Compiègne

1431   January: Joan's trial begins at Rouen
        May: Joan executed

1431   Council of Basel (1431–1449)

1435   Treaty of Arras

1436   Paris pledges fealty to Charles VII

1449   French regain Rouen

1450   Gutenberg sets up workshop for printing press

1453   July: Battle of Castillon
        End of the Hundred Years' War
        Ottoman Turks capture Constantinople

1456   Joan's Trial of Rehabilitation

1558   English lose Calais

1920   Joan canonized a saint

Part One

Historical Context

My heart beats wildly,

    I cannot be still;

For I myself have heard the blast of the horn,

    the battle cry.

Ruin upon ruin is reported;

    the whole land is laid waste.

In an instant my tents are ravaged;

    in a flash, my shelters.

            Jeremiah 4:19–20

1

Charles, Dauphin of France (1428)

It seemed to Charles VII and most of his contemporaries in 1428 that the famed four horsemen of the apocalypse—war, famine, conquest, and death—had swept through Europe for more than a century and were now outside of the walls of Orléans with the English army besieging one of France's most important cities. In 1425, the renowned and much-feared Duke of Bedford, younger brother of the dead king Henry V of England and regent of France for his son, the child-king Henry VI (1421–1471), returned to his native soil to settle an internal dispute among his countrymen. His absence, however, brought no advantage to Charles. By March 1427, Bedford was back in France with a plan to end a long, drawn-out conflict between England and France that had begun in 1337. If he could gain control of Orléans on the Loire River to use as a base of operations, he and his Burgundian allies could destroy opposition from the dauphinists and end Charles' aspiration of being crowned King of France, thus cementing the kingship of France for young Henry VI of England.

Keeping Orléans in the dauphinist cause was critical for Charles. The besieging force under the Earl of Salisbury was small—only about four thousand men—but the threat was existential and potentially catastrophic. Charles considered taking refuge in Scotland, but a prophecy had been circulating throughout the French countryside of a maiden who would come from God and turn the tide of war toward the loyalists. There was also news from the garrison town of Vaucouleurs of a young girl who claimed to be on a mission from God to crown the dauphin king and drive the English from France for good. Perhaps Charles wondered if God might finally drive the English from his realm along with the four horsemen through this young maiden and once again restore peace to a land that had known more than its fair share of sorrow over the past century.

2

A Century of Sorrows
The Great Famine (1315 to 1322)

It was as if Europe were being primed for a disaster. The convergence of a number of propitious factors throughout Europe from the tenth century through the thirteenth century led to political stability, improved agricultural production, and population growth. The feudal system had matured over the five hundred years since the dissolution of the Roman Empire, and it was now able to provide a stable form of government and social structure. The Church had also developed as an institution and the clergy had risen to prominence, contributing a spiritual arm of governance that complemented the secular arm of royalty and nobility. Agricultural production increased as the climate in Europe became warmer, and ample rains fell. Forests were cleared and swamps were drained and made useful for farming.

The increase in the food supply along with political and economic stability helped to fuel a population explosion that lasted into the fourteenth century. Europe's population doubled between 1000 and 1300. Towns grew, trade increased, and cities became larger and more prosperous. The beginnings of a middle class appeared in Europe as the number of merchants increased along with their wealth, and skilled artisans formed trade guilds and demanded representation in local government. Schools and universities were founded and grew in prestige and importance, and ancient Greek and Arabic texts were made available thanks to Islamic scholars living in Spain. Warfare continued, and there were food shortages and other hardships, but medieval society from the tenth century into the fourteenth century was blessed with growth, wealth, political and economic stability, and an increase in the standard of living.

Then the weather changed.

Europeans began noticing colder weather and more rainfall in the early 1300s. The year 1315 saw an exceptionally wet spring, which caused fields to go unplowed. In those that were, heavy rains drowned planted seed and rotted sprouting shoots, causing a dramatic decrease in the food supply. Animals suffered along with their human masters and herds were depleted due to starvation and disease. People fed themselves by hunting, foraging, eating their livestock, and consuming next year's supply of seed grain. The rains continued through 1316 and abated somewhat in the summer of 1317, but parts of Europe had flooded, especially near coastal areas, causing displaced populations to wander throughout the countryside and into cities in search of food and employment. The winters remained unseasonably cold for at least another decade and the Baltic Sea froze over at least twice. Parts of the North Sea were frozen as well.

By 1325, the food supply had returned to adequate levels, but "the Great Famine," as it came to be known, caused disruptions to European society that lasted for decades, and its effects were only worsened by war. Those who did not die from starvation by 1325 suffered from malnutrition and a weakened immune system. This left them vulnerable to disease, which would have dire consequences when the bubonic plague struck Europe in 1347.

3

A Century of Sorrows
The Hundred Years' War (1337 to 1347)

When Duke William of Normandy claimed the crown of England at the death of the last Anglo-Saxon king, Edward the Confessor, and then defeated his Anglo-Saxon rival, Harold Godwinsson, at the Battle of Hastings on October 14, 1066, a complicated relationship developed between the kings of England and France. The King of England, by virtue of the fiefs he held in France, became the vassal of the King of France, resulting in an uneasy detente that lasted for almost two hundred years. Tension between the monarchs reached a peak, however, when Henry Plantagenet, vassal to the King of France as the Duke of Normandy, Count of Anjou, and Duke of Aquitaine, became Henry II, King of England in 1154. It did not help matters that Henry had married the King of France's recently divorced ex-wife, Eleanor, in order to gain the duchy of Aquitaine.

A protracted struggle over the next hundred years culminated in 1259 with the Treaty of Paris, by which time King Henry III of England had lost much of the land formerly held by his predecessors. The quarrel continued with their royal successors, however, even if it was allayed somewhat by the Treaty of Amiens in 1279 and the Treaty of Paris in 1286. But rule over the duchy of Guyenne remained a source of unease and at times open hostility. Philip IV, "the Fair," of France (r. 1285–1314) took possession of most of Guyenne between 1294 and 1297, and the duchy was again invaded by Charles of Valois in 1324 and 1325.

Edward II of England responded by appointing his thirteen-year-old son, Edward, as the Duke of Guyenne in 1325, but after the king was deposed and murdered by his wife Isabella and her lover Mortimer in 1327, the young Edward became king. He was fifteen years old at the time of his accession, but it was Queen Isabella and Roger de Mortimer, Earl of March, who were the power behind the throne. This lasted until 1330 when Edward III, now eighteen years old and chafing under the control of the queen mother and her lover, was ready to rule in his own right. Edward had Mortimer hanged and consigned his mother to castle imprisonment.

Two years prior to this, the last Capetian king of France, Charles IV, died in 1328 without a male heir. His wife Jeanne was pregnant at the time of his death but she bore a daughter, which brought the Capetian line to an end. Edward III, then sixteen, was Charles' nephew and the son of his sister Isabella, who was the daughter of King Philip IV. Edward, or more accurately Isabella, Mortimer, and their advisors, used this as justification to claim the throne of France for Edward. This was entirely unacceptable to the French barons, however, and instead of Edward they chose Charles' cousin, Philip, Duke of Valois (Philip VI, r. 1328–1350), who was serving as regent until Jeanne gave birth. There were no specific rules at the time regarding the succession to the throne of France through a female line, but the French nobles could not bear to be ruled by Queen Isabella and her lover Mortimer, nor did they wish to be ruled by a king of another realm. Philip, thirty-five years old, was twenty years older than Edward and one of their own. His accession began a line of thirteen kings of the Valois dynasty which lasted until 1589.

Edward III, still under the control of Isabella and Mortimer in 1328 and only in his mid-teens, was forced to do homage for Guyenne at a ceremony in Amiens in 1329. Once Edward removed Isabella and Mortimer from power in 1330, and after having dealt with civil unrest from Mortimer's disaffected followers, he marched on the city of Berwick in Scotland and defeated the Scottish army at Halidon Hill in 1334. In his ranks were rows of archers—ordinary foot soldiers—fighting alongside professionally trained knights. Edward's archers were armed with a revolutionary weapon, the longbow, which would help the English achieve stunning victories over the French during the next hundred years and tilt the balance of power in their favor. The Welsh used them in the service of Edward I, who developed them for use in the Scottish Highlands.

The longbow was a revolutionary development in the history of weaponry on the order of the Egyptian chariot, Greek sarissa,

Roman gladius, stirrup, and cannon. It took years to fully train a longbowman, but a skilled one could deliver six to twelve arrows a minute. It had a range of two to three hundred yards and could pierce armor, which gave ordinary foot soldiers an advantage over knights. The longbow was particularly effective against mounted knights, as volleys of arrows would rain down upon the backs of their horses, killing or disabling them or putting them into a panic.

The French did not deploy archers with longbows but used crossbows instead, whose usual rate of fire was only two bolts a minute. The Battle of Halidon Hill was a preview of the battles that would be fought in France during the Hundred Years' War in which the longbow played a decisive role in the crushing English victories.

It was around 1325 that gunpowder was first used in battle, but early models of cannon were unreliable, dangerous to use, and generally ineffective against their targets. It took another hundred years for the technology of cannonry to develop, but once cannons became effective against stone walls, castles and the walled fortifications surrounding cities eventually became obsolete. In 1375, the French employed forty cannons while besieging a fortress on the coast of Normandy. Their guns could not bring down the fortifications, but the bombardment eventually forced the English garrison to surrender. At the Battle of Castillon in 1453, French forces used field artillery extensively for the first time with devastating effect on the English.[2] In the

---

[2] Castillon marked the end of the Hundred Years' War.

same year, the once-impregnable walls of Constantinople were finally breached by the Ottoman Turks with the aid of one of the largest cannons ever forged. If it were not for the development of superior cannonry, the city might still be named after its founder and its residents still speaking primarily Greek.

In 1336, Philip sailed the French fleet into the English Channel and threatened an invasion. In 1337, he confiscated the duchy of Guyenne from Edward, who responded by asserting his right to the throne of France in a letter sent to Philip on October 7, 1337. Thus began a war of intermittent battles between England and France that would last for more than a century.

While historians date the beginning of the Hundred Years' War by convention to 1337, the origins of this conflict can be traced to the Battle of Hastings in 1066. The first phase of what actually became a 116-year struggle lasted for the duration of Edward III's reign until his death in 1377, at which time England had very few territorial possessions in France despite all of Edward's military and diplomatic endeavors.

This first phase began with naval battles and Edward's efforts to gain allies in Europe. He initially sought an alliance with Flanders, but Louis I, Count of Nevers, was a vassal to Philip VI of France and would not betray his lord. Edward instead turned to Jacob van Artevelde, a wealthy brewer of Ghent, with whom he formed an alliance in 1340. Edward then placed an embargo on English wool to the cities of Flanders, which caused much disruption to the Flemish economy since Flanders' textile industry was heavily dependent on it. Under Artevelde's leadership, the merchants rebelled against Louis in 1340 and recognized Edward's claim to the kingship of France. That same year, Edward formally assumed the title of King of France.

Edward had spent much of England's resources in his struggle against Philip, and he was forced to pawn his crown and leave his wife and children in Ghent as collateral for a loan he used to finance his next military campaign in France. He attempted to draw Philip into battle when he marched an English army supported by Flemish allies from Flanders into France, burning, pillaging, and killing French civilians. Philip, respected as a warrior in his time, marched a French army north to meet Edward, but after first accepting battle, he declined and withdrew his forces. Edward was wasting time and money in his quest for a decisive victory and his Flemish allies began to demur. He sailed back to England and asked Parliament to levy new taxes. Parliament was hesitant but did so because of the threat of invasion posed by the French fleet stationed at the port of Sluys, now joined by Castilian and Genoese ships.[3] Edward then directed his efforts toward a naval confrontation.

With the king personally in command, a small fleet of English cogs loaded with longbowmen and men-at-arms departed on June 22, 1340. On the following day, it sailed directly into France's larger navy at the port of Sluys and defeated it. The English

---

[3] One of the unintended consequences of these events was that Parliament's power to control taxation increased.

archers proved as effective at sea as they were on land, but while the Battle of Sluys was a glorious victory for England, it had little strategic effect. Edward was still hampered by debt as many of his subjects refused to pay the tax levied by Parliament. Moreover, he could not follow his naval victory at Sluys with one on land since Philip wisely declined to give battle when Edward reentered France at the head of an army. As his allies began to peel away, and unable to force a decisive encounter, Edward reluctantly agreed to the Truce of Espléchin in 1340, which he saw as no more than a respite to marshal his resources for a future attempt at the French throne.

Edward's financial woes spilled over into other aspects of the European economy with disastrous results. The proceeds he expected from the wool tax were insufficient, which caused him to default on some of his loans. This had a ruinous effect on the Bardi and Peruzzi banking firms of Florence, both of which failed, wrecking Florence's economy. Had Edward borne the full cost of the war, it would have ended any hope he had harbored for the French throne and may have preempted the territorial ambitions of future English kings in France, but Edward's greed for land and kingship was not satiated, and undaunted and unruined, he planned his next move against Philip.

With new subsidies voted by Parliament in 1345, Edward assembled another army and navy and landed fifteen thousand men, including four thousand archers, in July 1346. Among his troops was his fifteen-year-old son, Edward of Woodstock, Prince of Wales, better known to history as "the Black Prince." Edward's army despoiled the Norman countryside, plundering and burning town after village, taking booty and holding hostages for ransom.

Philip had previously sent an army led by his son, John of Normandy, to Guyenne to deal with Edward's cousin, Henry, Duke of Lancaster. John was besieging the city of Aiguillon when Edward invaded Normandy, so Philip gathered another army and marched to confront Edward. Edward was attempting to evade Philip and join forces with his Flemish allies when Philip caught up with the English at Crécy near the Somme River on August 25. Both armies prepared for battle.

Edward had the advantage of choosing the ground, and he chose well. His army was situated atop a hill with a river protecting its right flank and a forest protecting its rear. On August 26, Philip was pressed to attack by his commanders against his better judgment. The king demurred as his troops were not entirely ready, but the overconfidence of the French nobility at Crécy in 1346 mirrored their superciliousness at Poitiers in 1356 and at Agincourt in 1415, and on each occasion, nemesis followed hubris. The English archers poured arrows down upon the French knights arrayed in formation and as they were charging up the hill. Those who made it to the top were met by relatively fresh English men-at-arms who dispatched them by the dozen. By the close of the day, the English had lost less than a hundred men while thousands of French knights and nobles littered the field.

Victory was complete and the consequences were devastating, even if Crécy was not strategically decisive. Confidence in the French king diminished and regard for the nobility, once viewed as an elite warrior class, ebbed after its decimation by ordinary foot soldiers. Taxation became more difficult, and these changing attitudes toward royalty and nobility were only enhanced by the outbreak of plague in 1347.

The Battle of Crécy cemented the longbowmen's place in the history of warfare. Yet despite his massive victory, Edward did not pursue his beaten opponent, nor did he march on Paris. His troops needed rest, so he marched on Calais and besieged it for almost a year before it finally succumbed due to a lack of provisions in August 1347. Philip marched an army to defend the city, but it was Edward's turn to refuse battle, and Philip could do no more than march his army home.

While the siege rewarded Edward with a walled city as a foothold in Europe, it was expensive in manpower, money, and provisions. Both kings now lacked the funds to continue active warfare, and the Black Death intervened anyway, making war impossible. It is notable at this stage of the war that after having won an important naval victory and an equally impressive land battle, no important strategic advantage came to Edward except the possession of the walled seaport of Calais.

4

A Century of Sorrows
The Black Death (1347 to 1351)

Originating somewhere in Asia, the bubonic plague was brought
to the Genoese trading town of Kaffa (now Feodosia) in the
Crimea by a Mongol army under the Khan Jani Beg. The Mongols
were laying siege to Kaffa, but because of an outbreak of the
plague within their ranks, the siege had to be lifted. The Mongol
army moved on from the Black Sea to Russia and India, carrying
the plague with them, but before they left Kaffa, they catapulted
infected corpses into the city, causing its population to become
infected. When the Genoese galleys departed Kaffa, the traders
brought the plague to Constantinople and Mediterranean ports in
Sicily and Italy. From there, it spread throughout Europe over a
period of four years, killing one-third of the population (twenty to
twenty-five million in Europe and as many in Asia and Africa)
from 1347 until 1351 when it finally subsided in the Scandinavian
countries. Other outbreaks occurred in 1361–63 (killing around
ten percent of the European population), 1369–71, 1374–75,
1390, and 1400.

While many at the time believed that "the pestilence" had been sent by God as a punishment for sin, it is now known that the bacteria *Yersinia pestis* infected fleas, which transmitted the plague to rats. When the host rat died, the fleas migrated to other rats. A bite from a flea or rat was enough to transmit the disease to humans and other animals, although bacilli could also be transmitted from human to human through pneumonic infection (i.e., a cough or sneeze). Once infected, most victims did not last long—from a matter of hours to a few days—although perhaps ten percent of those infected managed to survive. The plague did most of its damage in a geographical location within a year, usually killing one-third of its inhabitants. Some towns and villages were entirely wiped out, but those that did not have extensive trade relations with other communities escaped relatively unscathed.

The Black Death[4] brought dramatic and enduring changes to European society. Medieval people were very religious, but many lost confidence in the Church because it seemed utterly powerless to stem the tide of contagion and death. Some priests abandoned their dying parishioners and their families for fear of contamination, while whole communities of monasteries and convents were wiped out, their prayers ineffectual at saving even their own lives. Pope Clement VI announced a holy year in 1350 and pilgrims were invited to Rome as a way to appease God's wrath, but the plague ravaged those in attendance, making the pope look weak and inept. Prayers, sacrifices, blessings,

---

[4] Medieval people did not use this term but referred to it as "the pestilence."

processions, flagellations, and lengthy vigils seemed to have no effect in persuading God to alleviate the suffering and loss of life. Superstition increased, and faithful Christians, doubting the efficacy of prayer to the saints, turned to folk remedies and amulets. The spiritual power of the Church, once a source of hope and strength, now appeared as an illusion. This change in the attitude toward the Church and religion would survive long past the outbreak of the plague.

Second, the proliferation of death put a higher value on the labor of those who survived. Prior to the Great Famine of 1315–1322, the population of Europe had steadily increased over the past three centuries, providing a plentiful labor force while keeping wages low. By the 1350s, the labor market was radically altered, as the demand for agricultural products decreased with the shrunken population and the labor value of skilled artisans increased. Serfs left their lords to find jobs in the relative freedom of towns and villages, and the value of land decreased as it became less productive due to the decline in the agricultural workforce. The nobility used their political power to pass laws restricting the movement of serfs and freezing wages at the pre-plague level. This caused widespread resentment that eventually led to the Jacquerie (peasant uprising) in France in 1358 and the Peasants' Revolt in England in 1381.

Third, highly populated areas were hardest hit by the plague, and many of their skilled artisans died. They were replaced by serfs who migrated from the countryside, but while the demand and prices of manufactured goods and luxury items remained high, the quality of the work was inferior. Even so, wealth flowed into towns and cities and away from the landed aristocracy, which made cities more powerful at the expense of rural nobility. This fueled an emerging middle class and added to the class conflict between nobles and laborers, and merchants and tradesmen.

Fourth, although the Church lost prestige because of its inability to curtail the plague, it became wealthier due to the contributions in land and other property bequeathed to it in the wills of faithful Christians. Yet a wealthier Church is not necessarily a holier Church, and this increase in affluence would have future ramifications in the Church's relationship with the powerful monarchs of Europe. In addition, although the Church became wealthier, the plague was most severe in densely populated communities, which made it particularly destructive to monasteries and convents as well as to parish priests who remained with their flocks until they became infected and died. The Church had not only lost respect but many of its members, which would weaken it in future conflicts with powerful monarchs who also benefited from the declining power of the nobility and the rising power of towns and cities. The increased power of kings at the expense of nobles and the Church meant less fragmentation in society and a greater centralization of power, and eventually led to the formation of modern nation-states.

The political and social changes caused by the Black Death made the plague a watershed moment in European history. Rarely do events occur that change the world almost overnight, but the Black Death was one of these, and more than any other cause, it brought about the end of the medieval period.

It also coincided with the beginning of what we today call the Renaissance. Historians distinguish between the Southern or Italian Renaissance, which began around the middle of the fourteenth century, and the Northern or German Renaissance, which occurred about a century later. Humanism and other Renaissance ideas pertaining to religion, government, economics, and national consciousness worked synergistically with the natural phenomenon of the plague and its aftermath to challenge feudal ideas and created an impetus for transition from the medieval to the modern world.

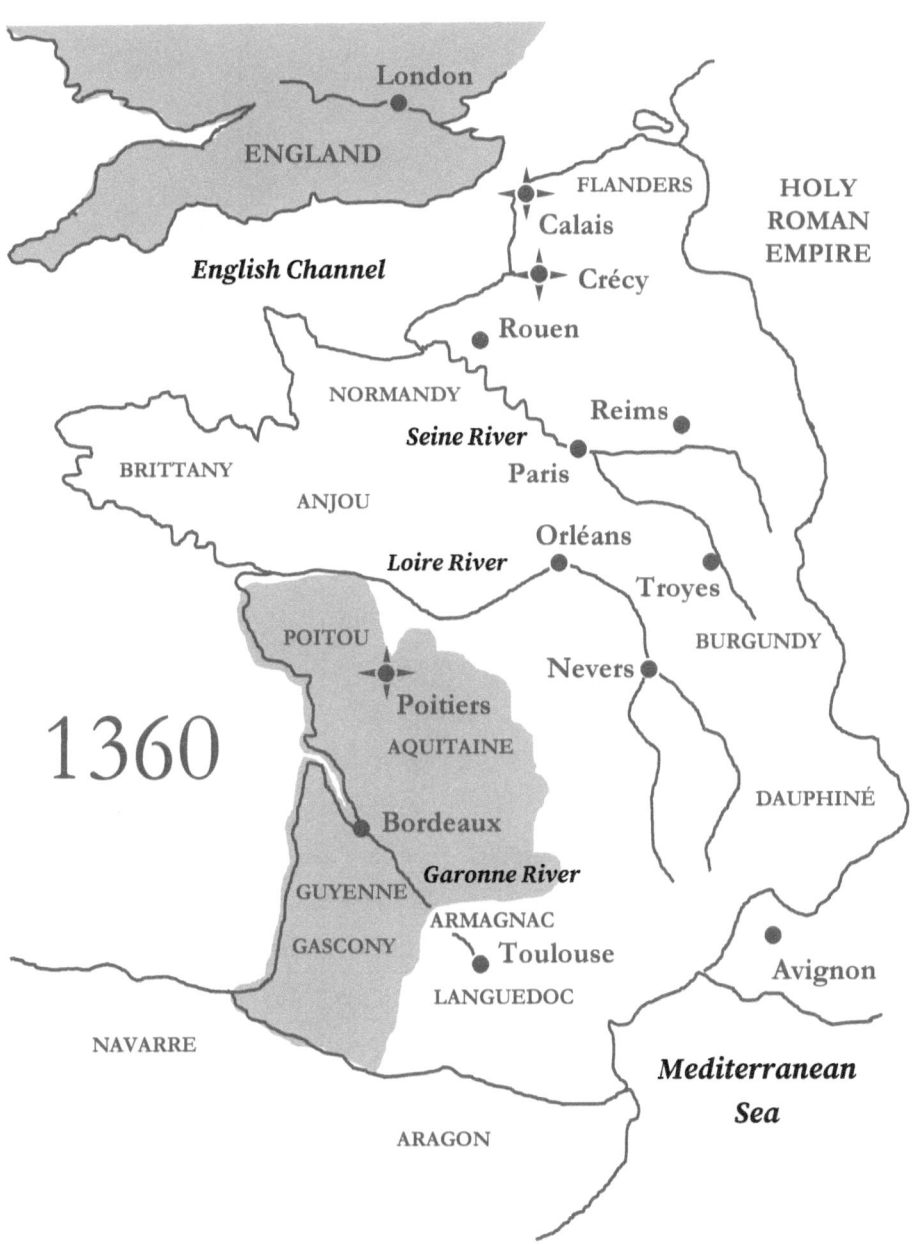

London

ENGLAND

English Channel

FLANDERS

HOLY
ROMAN
EMPIRE

Calais

Crécy

Rouen

NORMANDY

Seine River

Reims

BRITTANY

Paris

ANJOU

Orléans

Loire River

Troyes

POITOU

BURGUNDY

1360

Poitiers

AQUITAINE

Nevers

Bordeaux

Garonne River

DAUPHINÉ

GUYENNE

ARMAGNAC

GASCONY

Toulouse

Avignon

NAVARRE

LANGUEDOC

Mediterranean
Sea

ARAGON

5

A Century of Sorrows
The Hundred Years' War (1355 to 1413)

It would take many years before Europe recovered from the Black Death, but Edward III's aspirations for the French throne, or at least sovereign rule over a large portion of France, would not be thwarted even by one of Europe's most devastating catastrophes. Philip VI died in 1350 and was replaced by his son, the Duke of Normandy, who was crowned John II. John almost immediately alienated the nobility by executing a popular noble, the Count of Eu, who had just returned from captivity in England, and replacing him as the Constable of France with his close associate, Charles of Spain. Next, he attempted to solve his fiscal problems by debasing the low-value coinage used in daily transactions, which had greater negative economic consequences for the average citizen than for the wealthy. John also awarded his new constable the county of Angoulême, which was part of Charles of Navarre's territory. In compensation for the loss, John offered Charles his eight-year-old daughter as a bride but then withheld the dowry. In revenge, Charles "the Bad" had Charles of Spain assassinated.

In addition to Navarre, Charles held fiefs in Normandy and central France, which made him a powerful ally, and the assassination of Charles of Spain drew other disaffected nobles to him. To increase pressure on John II and to protect and expand his territorial possessions, Charles began negotiations with Edward toward an alliance. Edward, however, could not afford further military operations and faced opposition from both Parliament and commoners who were weary of supporting a war that was neither profitable nor would end. John II was also limited by insubstantial funds and by the potential disloyalty of Charles of Navarre and was forced to swallow his pride and publicly reconcile with him in 1354. Through the mediation of the pope, Edward and John began peace negotiations, but these ended in failure because the proposed treaty was far too favorable toward the English.

Charles again approached Edward about an alliance and then vigorously denied it to the pope. Edward once again declared to Parliament and the English people that the French had wronged him and he was able to raise enough money for another expedition on the continent. The truce that was in effect expired, and in 1355 the English transported two armies into France. The first was led by the king's son, Edward, Prince of Wales and the recently appointed Duke of Guyenne, and the other by Henry, Duke of Lancaster. The prince's army laid waste to a swath of land from Bordeaux to Narbonne and back again, a campaign that could only be described as a medieval version of terrorism meant to break the will of the French people, destroy resources that could be used to wage war, and create opposition to John II that would force him into a peace settlement favorable to the English. The army under Lancaster met John's army near Amiens, but no battle ensued.

Again in 1356, the English took the field with two armies, but John burned the bridges that crossed the Loire River to prevent them from joining forces. He marched an army toward Lancaster and drove him off, and then turned south to confront Edward, finally overtaking him near Poitiers. John was not known in his time as a capable captain of war, but his army was larger than Edward's. The pope sent a representative to mediate between the two sides and a truce was declared for one day (Sunday), which gave time for the English to improve their defensive position. Edward offered to make significant concessions, but negotiations broke down when he was told he would have to surrender himself as a prisoner. Both sides prepared for battle the following day.

The French high command was divided between besieging the English and forcing a pitched battle. Against the advice of some of his counselors, John stubbornly opted for battle. Encircling the English and waiting for them to starve and surrender would have been more strategically prudent, but battle was more honorable to the medieval mind than siege warfare. On Monday, September 19, the two armies engaged in a day-long struggle that resembled the

Battle of Crécy and ended in an equally crushing French defeat. To compound French misfortune, John II was captured and became a prisoner of the King of England.

The core of France was shaken. Popular resentment of the royalty and nobility by commoners after Poitiers exceeded the resentment felt after Crécy. Many important nobles were taken prisoner along with the king, each held for ransom that would in large part be paid by the work of peasants. The central government, now led by the eighteen-year-old dauphin, was in complete disorder, and the English were in position to drive a hard bargain. A two-year truce was arranged, during which time negotiations would take place. Mercenary bands of unemployed soldiers from various parts of Europe, called Free Companies,[5] remained in France and roamed around the countryside pillaging, destroying, and creating havoc and misery. To make matters worse, Charles of Navarre, who had been imprisoned by John in 1356, escaped in September 1357 and began conspiring to be king in opposition to Charles the dauphin.

In May 1358, under the weight of heavy taxation and because of the intense suffering inflicted on them by marauding Free Companies, French peasants rebelled in desperation. Some committed atrocities even worse than those of the Free Companies. The Jacquerie revolt was soon crushed by the nobility, however, and Charles the Bad, who had helped to suppress the uprising, again conspired with the King of England

---

[5] *Écorcheurs*, brigands, freebooters, marauders, "fleecers."

while negotiations were proceeding with John II and the French government. One treaty was proposed, but Edward was too greedy to accept it. He offered another proposal in March 1359, but it was refused by the French Estates General, and Edward used this as a pretext for another invasion of France. He was allied with Charles of Navarre, but when Charles learned that Edward wanted to be crowned King of France, he switched sides and made peace with the dauphin in August 1359.

Edward landed in Calais and marched south attempting to draw the dauphin and his army into the open field for battle, but the dauphin refused. The campaign ended in 1360 with the Treaty of Brétigny in which Edward renounced his claim to the French throne in return for greatly expanded territorial possessions held in full sovereignty. John's ransom was set at three million gold crowns and he was allowed to return to France. The terms of the treaty were never fulfilled, however, so John voluntarily returned to England in 1364 and died soon after at age forty-five. The dauphin was crowned as Charles V. He opposed the Treaty of Brétigny, which meant the conflict between England and France would continue. Charles was not a warrior, and he concentrated his efforts instead on diplomacy while leaving military decisions to his commanders in the field.

In 1368, the lords of Guyenne, who had long been loyal to English rule, appealed to King Edward and King Charles about the heavy taxation that the Black Prince had imposed upon their fiefs. Charles accepted their appeals and prepared for war. Edward considered this a breach of treaty, and hostilities resumed. By 1370, the French had built up their forces and were able to win important battles in northern France under their new constable, Bertrand du Guesclin, and a French-Castilian fleet defeated the English navy off La Rochelle in 1372. But English armies still roamed the countryside, and in one particularly cruel incident even by the standards of the day, the Black Prince massacred three thousand civilians at Limoges in revenge for their disloyalty. This was his last act of war, however, as he contracted dysentery and was forced to return to England in 1372. There he remained an invalid until his death on June 8, 1376, a year before his father Edward's death on June 21, 1377.

King Charles continued to make diplomatic progress, and by 1374, he had reacquired most of the land lost to England since the outbreak of the Hundred Years' War. The kingdom of France might have expelled the English from the continent entirely, but the French were exhausted, their king in poor health, and its treasury depleted. The English too were spent. Edward had become an alcoholic, and his heir, the Black Prince, was an invalid. The next in line for the throne was the prince's young son, and upon the deaths of his father and grandfather in 1377, Richard II (r. 1377–1399) was crowned king at the age of ten. In 1380, Charles V of France died along with his constable and was succeeded by his twelve-year-old son, Charles VI (r. 1380–1422).

Since both countries had boy-kings, the task of governing fell to their elders who competed against each other for greater power.

A council led by the Dukes of Burgundy, Berry, and Anjou was established to serve as Charles' regency. From 1379 to 1383, Philip van Artevelde led revolts in Flanders against Louis de Mâle, Count of Flanders. When Louis died in 1384, possession of Flanders, along with Artois, passed to Charles' uncle, Philip the Bold, Duke of Burgundy. This would have great consequences in the future when the struggle for power between powerful French nobles would turn deadly and eventually evolve into a civil war.

England during Richard's early reign was troubled by the threat of invasion and raids on its southern coast by French and Castilian ships. In response, Parliament authorized additional taxes to raise funds for defensive measures, which prompted English peasants to revolt in 1381 just as French peasants had rebelled in 1358. The Peasants' Revolt was not precipitated solely by heavy taxation, however. Feudal society was evolving in the aftermath of the Black Death, and ideas about class superiority in the medieval caste system were being questioned in England as well as in France. This development was strengthened by the success of ordinary soldiers against noble men-at-arms at Crécy and Poitiers. The Peasants' Revolt seriously challenged the status quo in England, but it was put down as ruthlessly as the Jacquerie had been in France, and its leaders were punished severely. Even though it was not ultimately successful, the Peasants' Revolt was another important event of the mid-to-late fourteenth century that signaled a period of transition in Europe from a medieval to an early modern society.

Eventually, Richard and Charles grew into manhood and sought to rule their respective realms on their own. Richard wanted peace and closer relations with France. Since both kingdoms were occupied with internal struggles and lacked the funds to pursue war, a truce was signed at Leulinghen in 1389 that suspended hostilities until 1403.

Richard's wife died in 1394, and in his desire for closer relations with France and its king, Richard proposed that he be given Charles' daughter Isabella as a bride even though he was thirty years old and she only six. The offer was accepted, and Richard and Charles also agreed to extend the truce of Leulinghen for twenty-eight years. The two kings met in Calais in 1396 amidst great rejoicing. Oaths of friendship and promises of fidelity were exchanged and peace between the two kingdoms might have followed if it were not for important English nobles who opposed Richard's policy. This caused Richard to become autocratic and heavy-handed, and he imprisoned and killed some of the nobles. When Richard went on campaign against Irish rebels in 1399, Henry Bolingbroke—named after the castle in which he was born—seized power. Richard and Henry were cousins born in the same year, 1367, and had spent their childhood together at court, but this did not prevent Henry from deposing and imprisoning Richard. Bolingbroke was crowned king in 1399 as Henry IV while Richard died in prison of starvation in 1400.

~

France's population was three times greater than England's during the period of the Hundred Years' War, and it had greater resources. Had France been united under its king and its nobility not been preoccupied with competition for power, it should have easily expelled the English. But France was divided, and it would eventually descend into civil war.

The episodes of madness that would plague Charles VI for the remainder of his life began in 1392. His bouts of insanity furthered a rivalry between the house of Orléans, led by Louis, Duke of Orléans, and the house of Burgundy, led by Philip the Bold. Both were powerful and ambitious uncles of the king and each strove to fill the power vacuum created by Charles' incapacitation. Philip died in 1404 and was replaced by his son, John the Fearless, as leader of the Burgundian faction. Burgundian influence in the French court increased and violent clashes ensued in the streets of Paris between Burgundian and Orléanist supporters. John sought to put an end to the feud by having Louis assassinated in Paris on November 23, 1407. This event marked the beginning of the French civil war.

Louis' murder created a power vacuum that was filled by Bernard of Armagnac, who served as regent for Louis' three young sons. The Orléanists faction thus became known as the Armagnacs, and also as the dauphinists because of their support for Charles VII. In addition, this party is also referred to as the nationalists because they resisted the English as foreign invaders and opposed the Anglo-Burgundian party which favored the English king.

John and the Burgundians were in the ascendant in 1408, but the Armagnacs sent an army to blockade Paris. Both sides reached out to Henry for assistance, and the King of England responded to John's request by sending 2,800 soldiers to Paris to help relieve the siege. Once it was lifted the English troops returned home, but another English army arrived at the request of the Armagnacs that pillaged its way through France. John the Fearless attempted to impose taxes in order to repel the English, but this only provoked violent resistance and John had to flee to Burgundy. Henry died in March 1413 and was succeeded by his son, Henry V, who became one of the most important figures in the Hundred Years' War and one of the most famous of all of England's kings.

6

A Century of Sorrows
The Avignon Papacy and the Western Schism

Hardship and division spared neither the secular nor the spiritual arm of European government during the fourteenth century. The dispute between France and England over control of French lands and the antagonism that emerged in medieval society as disillusioned commoners gained greater independence from their lords was mirrored in the Church by another form of division. In 1309, Pope Clement V (r. 1305–1314) relocated from Rome to Avignon, where he attempted to govern the Church and the Papal States. This arrangement lasted until 1377 and proved costly in lives and treasure. To make matters worse, the papacy itself was divided between two and then three claimants from 1378 until 1415. The unruliness of the Roman mob and the interminable violence in Roman politics served as a pretext for Clement's decision, but the impetus for the Avignon Papacy and the Western Schism had deeper roots.

The eleventh and twelfth centuries saw a power struggle between Church and state in which the Church gained some degree of supremacy. During the reign of Pope Innocent III (r. 1198–1216), the papacy developed into a monarchy that wielded considerable secular power. The Church was already in possession of significant landholdings and had its own judicial and legislative systems, but the papacy gained more power during Innocent's reign and it competed more directly with rulers in the secular realm. As a result, it became a victim of its own success by becoming a target of criticism that diminished the Church's spiritual authority. Matters were complicated by the increasing politicization of the papacy and the upper echelons of Church hierarchy. Papal elections were routinely subject to interference and at times violent coercion. Powerful families in Italy dominated the Italian political scene, employed mobs to influence papal elections, and manipulated popes once they were in office.

By the end of the thirteenth century, the state of affairs in Europe had changed. The kings of England and France had grown stronger and more independent from Rome and were less hesitant to assert what they viewed as their right to land, power, and taxation. Theory on the rights of spiritual authority in relation to secular authority came under scrutiny. Boniface VIII (r. 1294–1303) became pope at a pivotal moment when the power of kings and the centralization of government was increasing. Clergy were being taxed in France and England to help fund military ventures in contradiction to Innocent's decree that they could not lawfully do so without the consent of the pope. In 1296, Boniface issued the papal bull *Clericis Laicos*, which defended the Church's liberty from secular taxation. King Edward I of England and King Philip

IV of France retaliated with measures of their own that caused Boniface to moderate his position.

In 1300, Boniface called the Church's first-ever jubilee year and pilgrims flocked to Rome by the thousands, emboldening the pope to reassert his authority in secular matters. Boniface declared that popes did not merely have the divine right to govern in coordination with secular authority, but that God had placed popes *over* all secular authority, thus making the whole secular realm subject to papal authority. In addition, Boniface issued the bull *Unam Sanctum* in 1302 in which he claimed that all human beings, when it comes to salvation, are subject to the pope. Philip responded by sending armed men into Italy to arrest and imprison Boniface, who would have been beaten to death had he not been saved by the local citizenry. He died in 1303 as a result of his wounds.

Competition for power between popes and kings continued after the relocation of the papal residence to Avignon. When Philip sought the treasure of the Knights Templar and demanded their suppression from Clement V and the Council of Vienne (1312–1314), they complied. Philip was present in Vienne during the council to make certain of the outcome, and it seemed his victory over the Church was complete.

All of the popes during the Avignon Papacy were French, which resulted in the appointment of an inordinate number of Frenchmen to the College of Cardinals, almost guaranteeing the next pope would be French. To the disedification of many observers, the papal court eschewed modesty and modeled itself on the courts of kings, gaining for itself a reputation for worldliness and dissipation. Papal taxes were increased and a palace was built at great expense for the pope and his entourage. Respect for the papacy waned as protest against its excesses and sensuality increased. In 1324, Marsilius of Padua completed *Defensor pacis*, which criticized the pope for his self-appointed role in secular government. Both he and William of Ockham, another critic of the papacy, were excommunicated by Pope John XXII. Later in the fourteenth century, the Oxford theologian John Wycliffe, who believed that clergy members and religious should practice austerity and simplicity of life, supported the English kings against the papal excesses of Avignon. The early fifteenth century saw a preview of the Protestant movement when John Hus, a disciple of John Wycliffe, was excommunicated in 1410 and executed in 1415. This caused a rebellion among his followers and a series of civil wars that foreshadowed the Wars of Religion fought during the sixteenth century.

Pope Urban V (r. 1362–1370) returned to Rome in 1367 but stayed for only three years before moving back to Avignon in 1370. His successor, Gregory XI (r. 1370–1378), acceded to international pressure and relocated the papal residence to Rome in 1377 during the War of the Eight Saints (1376–1378) between the papacy and Florence. After Gregory's death in 1378, one of the most fateful papal elections in Church history took place when, under duress from the Roman mob, the cardinals elected an Italian archbishop, Urban VI (r. 1378–1389), as the new pope.

Urban was cordial and mild-mannered prior to his election, but a dramatic change in his personality occurred once he assumed office. Urban became hostile toward the French cardinals and publicly chastised them for their luxuriousness and decadent lifestyles. Fearing a loss of power or worse, the cardinals fled to Avignon, declared the election invalid, and elected one of their own, a Frenchman who took the name Clement VII (r. 1378–1397). Thus began the Western Schism, which lasted until 1415.

In 1054, the Great Schism between the Latin Church in the West and the Greek Church in the East caused great disruption within the Christian world. Europe descended into another disastrous split in 1378, not only within Christianity, but along national and political lines as well. England and its allies supported Urban VI in Rome, while France and its allies backed Clement VII in Avignon. Further division was added when proponents of the conciliar movement argued that ecumenical councils had more power than the pope and could depose and elect a pope. Those who favored papal supremacy argued that a pope's power derived directly from God and only a pope had the power to summon an ecumenical council.[6]

In 1398, in an effort to solve the problem of multiple popes, the French Church withdrew its obedience to Pope Benedict XIII

---

[6] The Catholic Church has since ruled that: (1) the pope alone has supreme power and authority within the Church, and (2) the legitimate line of popes was based in Rome, and therefore Urban VI and his successors were the rightful popes.

(r. 1394–1423), but he refused to abdicate and was not expelled from Avignon until 1403. In 1409, the Council of Pisa adopted the conciliar approach and deposed both rival popes and elected Alexander V. Unfortunately, neither of the other two popes resigned, so there were three popes from 1409 until 1415. Alexander died in 1410 and John XXIII was elected by the Council of Pisa in his place. John was urged to convoke the Council of Constance in 1414. This council deposed John, accepted the resignation of Gregory XII, declared the claim of Benedict XIII to be invalid, and elected Martin V as the sole pope.

The era of the Avignon Papacy and the Western Schism had finally come to an end in 1417 after more than a century of division. Its effects on the Church's reputation were to be permanent, however, and it never truly recovered from the loss of esteem it suffered from: (1) its inability to alleviate the misery caused by the Black Death, (2) the prevalent view that the papacy had overstepped its authority in secular matters, (3) the worldliness of the papal court and other members of Church hierarchy and religious orders, and 4) the dislocation of the pope from Rome and the schism between competing popes.

~

An understanding of the history of this unfortunate era is helpful when trying to gain insight into the mindset of Joan's judges at her trial in 1431. Church officials were sensitive to the loss of reputation they had suffered since 1309, and to some extent these events shed light on, but in no way justify, why her judges were so insistent that she submit to their authority.

7

A Century of Sorrows
Byzantine Civil Wars and the Ottoman Invasion

The Ottoman Empire creaked into the twentieth century, aged and decaying, until it finally met its demise in 1922 after siding with Germany and Austria-Hungary during World War I. On the whole, though, it enjoyed a lengthy and prosperous existence relative to other empires in history, and much to the uneasiness of late medieval Christians, it was able to extend its dominion onto the eastern shores of Europe.

The Turkish tribe known as the Osmanlis, named after their leader Osman[7] (r. 1290–1326), first appears in the historical record at the Battle of Bapheus in 1302 when, according to a Byzantine historian, he led the Turks in a victory over a Byzantine force. The Osmalis were only one among many Turcoman tribes and a minor power in Asia Minor at this time, but 151 years after Osman's victory at Bapheus, one of Osman's successors would control lands on the European and Asian sides of the Bosporus and finally

---

[7] From whom we also derive the name "Ottoman."

achieve the long-sought-after goal of capturing Constantinople and making it the capital of the empire.

A number of factors aided the remarkable rise of the Osmalis during the fourteenth century. First, the Byzantine Empire experienced a period of internal strife that resulted in sporadic civil war. The first of these was fought between 1321 and 1328, and the second between 1341 and 1347 after the death of Emperor Andronicus. Osmanli expansion was further aided by the antagonism that had long existed between Rome and Latin Christianity on one hand, and Constantinople and the Greek Orthodox Church on the other. Paramount in this conflict was the Fourth Crusade when in 1204 the Crusaders, instigated by Venice, overcame Constantinople's formidable defenses and irreligiously sacked the city. It remained under Western rule until 1261 when the exiled emperor, Michael Palaeologus, was able to regain control of it with Genoa's assistance. Constantinople never truly recovered from this sacking and occupation, though, and the Fourth Crusade remains to this day a source of friction between Eastern and Western Christianity.

Counterpoised to Byzantium as the other great civilization in the region at this time was the Arab-occupied lands to the south. When the Arabs under Mohammed stormed out of the Arabian Desert to spread Islam during the seventh century, their success was facilitated by the wars between the Byzantines and Persians, which exhausted both. In the same manner, Ottoman rise to power was bolstered by the Mongol invasion of Arab-held lands, which depleted the strength of Arab forces. Resistance to Ottoman expansion was further neutralized by Ottoman acceptance of Islam in the early fourteenth century.

Soon after their conversion, the Ottomans began to absorb Greek lands into their domain. Their first conquest was the town of Brusa in 1326, whose commander, Evrenos, willingly yielded to Osman and later became a Muslim. Osman died soon after taking Brusa and was succeeded by his son Orkhan, who made Brusa his capital. Orkhan was able to bring other Greek territories under Ottoman rule, and in 1331 he seized Nicaea, where over a thousand years earlier Constantine had called an ecumenical council out of which came the foundational Nicene Creed (325). In 1333, the Byzantines were forced to pay tribute to the Ottomans. During the Byzantine civil war fought between 1342 and 1347, the Ottomans formed an alliance with the new emperor, John VI Cantacuzenus, against his rival the Palaeologi, and Orkhan was given John's daughter, Princess Theodora, as a bride in 1346.

Orkhan and the Ottoman Turks caused Western Christianity alarm when in 1353 they captured Gallipoli on the European side of the Bosporus. The Ottomans crossed the Aegean Sea from Asia Minor at the invitation of John VI, who wished to weaken his rival, and moved to extend their dominion into Thrace. This caused great consternation in Europe, but because Europeans were debilitated from so many other calamities during the fourteenth century, no effective force could be mustered except Slavic and Greek forces already in the Balkans.

The Turks also benefited when Stefan Dušan, ruler of Serbia and an important defender of Europe against the Turks, died in 1355. In 1359, Orkhan died and was succeeded by his son Murad, who is considered by many historians to be the true founder of the Ottoman Empire. Murad promptly seized Adrianople, one of the most important cities in Byzantium, in 1361. Ten years later, he defeated the Serbs at the River Marica. Byzantium's second largest city, Thessalonica, fell in 1387, and in 1389 the Ottomans defeated the Serbs in the Battle of Kossova putting an end to Serbian independence. Murad died during the battle and was succeeded by his son, Bayazid.

The rapid advance of Islamic Turks on the eastern border of Europe distressed European Christians, but Bayazid, after placating the Slavs and consolidating his holdings in Europe, turned his attention east to Asia Minor. Sigismund marched at the head of a Hungarian army into Bulgaria, however, which caused Bayazid to turn back to protect his European territories. He defeated Sigismund and absorbed Bulgaria into his dominion, and then turned his eyes toward Constantinople. Although the Byzantines had given him no good reason, Bayazid besieged the city—the first time a Turkish ruler had attempted to do so. With the help of Genoa and Venice, and because of its formidable defensive walls (some of which still stand today), Constantinople was able to withstand the siege until it was finally lifted.

The ancient Greeks taught that nemesis follows upon hubris, and if the failed siege of Constantinople was a sign of hubris, then the ill-conceived manner in which Bayazid handled an incursion into Asia Minor by Timur (Tamerlane) in 1402 brought with it the unmistakable manifestation of nemesis. Tactical, strategic, and diplomatic mistakes resulted in a rout of Ottoman forces at the Battle of Ankara. Bayazid was captured and made a prisoner, and died shortly afterward.[8]

The defeat at Ankara did not slow Ottoman expansion, however. Slav soldiers and the Balkan provinces remained loyal to the Turks, and Timur did not follow up his victory with further campaigns into Asia Minor. In May 1453, the Ottomans under Sultan Mehmed II, armed with an enormous cannon and aided by recent advances in gunpowder, finally breached the hitherto impenetrable western walls of Constantinople and took the city. In July of that same year, French forces used a preponderance of field artillery for the first time with great effect against the English at the Battle of Castillon, finally putting an end to the Hundred Years' War. Gunpowder had come of age, and it helped propel a rapid transition from medieval to modern warfare.

Mehmed made Constantinople his capital, and the Hagia Sophia, the great Christian basilica built by Justinian in 537, became a mosque. Ironically, Western Christianity, which failed to

---

[8] Icarus should have listened to his father Daedalus and taken the middle course, or golden mean, which is where Aristotle said that virtue lies, but the youth became arrogant and learned his lesson the hard way.

provide adequate assistance to Constantinople in its battle with Islam, profited from the fall of Constantinople by receiving Greek scholars who fled from their Turkish conquerors. These scholars brought valuable Greek manuscripts to the West that contributed to the education of Europe and the budding of the period we know as the Renaissance.

8

A Century of Sorrows
The Rigors of Medieval Life

The vast majority of medieval people, perhaps ninety percent, were of the peasant class, lived in or near a village, and worked in agriculture. Their lives were governed by the Church, their lord, and the annual cycle of planting and harvesting. Life in the Middle Ages could be precarious, and one bad harvest could mean starvation and poverty.

Yet for all the labor and hardship that farming entailed, the diet of most peasants[9] lacked diversity and was unevenly distributed throughout the year. Many peasants survived on porridge, soup, stew, and coarse, unleavened black bread made from wheat, rye, and oatmeal. Vegetables were available part of the year, but serfs rarely ate meat until the late fourteenth century when meat, especially pork, became a regular part of their diet. Cow, sheep, and goat milk could be acquired year-round. Fish

---

[9] Also called "serfs" or "villeins."

might be on the menu, as would rabbit, fowl, and other game that peasants were permitted by their lords to hunt.

Women had a subordinate role in all ranks of medieval society. Peasant women worked in various occupations, such as domestic chores, spinning or mending clothes, taking care of small children, tending to the vegetable garden or livestock, and engaging in a skilled craft or trade. Making clothes took a great deal of time, as did food production, acquiring drinkable water, the construction and repair of homes and other buildings, tool repair, and procuring firewood for the hearth. Medieval clothing was rarely made of cotton since it had to be imported and was difficult to spin using the methods available at the time. Clothes were either made of wool—a popular trading commodity that constituted a major industry—and linen made from flax fibers. Very few peasants owned more than two sets of clothes.

The castles and manors of kings and nobles could be spacious and luxurious by medieval standards, but for the average peasant, life indoors meant a one- or two-room wooden dwelling with a dirt floor. Animals lived nearby and sometimes within the family home, which was always susceptible to fire. Tradesmen and artisans who depended on the use of fire had to be particularly careful. The windows were small and the light inside dim, even during the day. Chimneys were uncommon in most peasant dwellings, and if the smoke from the fire in the hearth could not escape through a passage or louver in the roof, it caused the interior to be smoky. Ventilation could be poor, and it was smelly inside since peasants bathed very infrequently, perhaps only once a year and sometimes not at all. It was also damp and usually cold, especially at night when the glowing embers in the hearth were too cool to provide any comfort. To relieve themselves, people went to outhouses built over pit latrines and wiped themselves with hay, straw, or grass.

Communal domestic life in medieval times meant that privacy, if there was any, was limited to sleeping alone, although most medieval people slept naked and often with other people in the bed. Sex took place in the midst of all. Public breastfeeding was not uncommon, and the familiarity medieval folk had with women's breasts and their communal mode of living explains why a number of fighting men with whom Joan served saw her breasts and commented that they were beautiful. This sounds strange to modern sensibilities, especially when Joan was so protective of her virginity, but life in medieval villages made such occurrences the norm.

As one might expect, peasants spent most of their lives outdoors, even if very few of them ever traveled very far from their village. Those who did sometimes went on pilgrimage to a site designated holy by the Church. For most peasants, this meant regional churches, cathedrals, or shrines, but those who could afford a longer journey made pilgrimages to Rome, Jerusalem, Santiago de Compostela, and Canterbury Cathedral. Reasons for undertaking pilgrimage varied: devotion, penance, obtaining a cure from disease, injury, or illness, or to request a favor for oneself or another, including deceased relatives. People during the Middle Ages also traveled for business and to attend the festivals and fairs that were so important to and characteristic of medieval life. These were more than a source of entertainment— they served as a holiday and the closest thing to a vacation that most medieval folk ever experienced.

As we have seen, the Black Death contributed to the growth of the middle class, mostly in cities and villages but also in the countryside. The famous English longbowmen, for example, were mostly yeomen who hired themselves out to the king during times of war. Within cities and villages, burghers—or townspeople who lived in a fortified enclosure—included middle-class merchants and skilled tradesmen. These burghers normally did not answer to a lord, but to a *burgermeister*, or mayor. Artisans and craftsmen had their own *cursus honorum*, which began with an apprenticeship (usually for boys), then journeyman status, and finally recognition as an expert or master. At this point they became members of a trade guild, the medieval version of a modern-day labor union.

Some of these tradesmen became wealthy, as did many of the merchants, especially those who traveled abroad. A rise in income and social status is often accompanied by an interest in education and demand for books. During the Early Middle Ages (c. 476– c. 1000 AD) and High Middle Ages (c. 1000–c. 1300), books were rare and usually only found in monasteries. During the Late Middle Ages (c. 1300–c. 1450), however, literacy increased and books and education became more widely available. All of this contributed to the rise in power of the middle class, and by 1454 when Johannes Gutenberg used the first movable type printing press to print the Bible, a growing literate populace was eager for the benefit of his revolutionary invention.

Despite this social progress, fourteenth- and fifteenth-century Europe remained a violent place. There will always be those in every society who gravitate toward military service, combat, and war by choice, but many young men in medieval society were pressed into such occupations by necessity. Farming methods had not advanced much since Roman times and were very inefficient by today's standards. Sons in peasant families whose land did not produce enough sustenance to support a growing household had little choice but to move on and sometimes sought employment as a soldier or mercenary. Likewise, sons of nobility who were not destined to inherit their fathers' land and property would often be trained as a knight. When they were of age, they left their fathers' estates to seek fortune elsewhere, and with any luck might gain a manor or duchy of their own.

Pitched battles between two large armies under a king or group of lords were rare in the Middle Ages, as such battles were expensive, risky, and unpredictable. The loss of manpower and horses, along with war materiel and hostages taken, served as a sufficient deterrent for such large-scale undertakings. Far more common were skirmishes, raids, pillaging, foraging, looting for plunder, and the taking of hostages for ransom. The Hundred Years' War saw much of this kind of warfare since it was effective in destroying local economies and caused much financial hardship to the French king and his lords. Castles were somewhat effective as a defense, but they were stationary and could not entirely solve the problem of roving bands of soldiers and mercenaries that played such a prominent and destructive role during the Hundred Years' War.

It was a small step for some to transition from serving in an organized army under a king or noble to reorganizing as a band of mercenaries under a captain when the lord was no longer in need of their services and disbanded his army. Even worse, they might reorganize as a gang of brigands, murderers, and thieves. Bands of men trained for combat with no other means of sustenance could easily use their martial skills for their own ends. Yesterday's company of soldiers fighting for a worthy cause or the rights of their lord could become today's highwaymen and village raiders, taking cover in the many woods and forests that covered the medieval landscape. Travel could be dangerous, especially alone or in a small group, which was another reason peasants remained close to their village.

Justice in the Middle Ages, when it could be found, was often violent and sometimes brutal. This is not to say that it was always fairly administered, as judges and sheriffs were susceptible to bribery and many became corrupt. When it was meted out, justice often came in the form of what we today would consider cruel and unusual. Those who were merely suspected of a crime were sometimes subject to severe trials to prove their innocence (i.e., combat, being tied and then thrown into water, or being exposed to fire or forced to pass through it). These trials were sometimes presided over by members of the Church hierarchy. If one was found guilty of a crime, he might be placed in a pillory or stocks, or tortured in any number of ways, sometimes leading to death, permanent disability, or disfigurement. If his offense were grave enough, he could be executed. Witches and heretics were burned at the stake, the fate that Joan was made to suffer.

Medieval people lived close to poverty. One unlucky break— a debilitating injury, the untimely death of a father or husband, a fire caused by a spark from the hearth or one that spread from a neighbor's home—could render a family destitute and dependent on the charity of others.

They also lived close to death. There was a high rate of child and teenage mortality during the Middle Ages, and those who lived into their sixties likely would have experienced much hardship, discomfort, and physical pain caused by injuries, illnesses, vermin, and disease. Medieval knowledge of medicine was limited. Surgery was rudimentary and featured blood-letting, and germ theory had not yet been proposed. There was a lack of hygiene and problems with sanitation disposal in the overcrowded streets of towns and cities. Everywhere, people lived amidst rats, fleas, mice, and lice. Eating raw or undercooked meat might lead to intestinal worms and other parasites. A lifetime of hard physical labor caused arthritis, and the lack of fruits and vegetables led to vitamin deficiency and scurvy. Loose, broken, and rotting teeth, oral hygiene that included no toothbrushes or toothpaste, human waste, animal waste, animal bites, and infection were a regular part of life. Roving armies and bands of freebooters were only one form of violence among many, and the lack of prisons and law enforcement officers meant that the regular occurrence of criminality made life even more tenuous and hazardous.

These were the times in which Joan lived. It is worth noting that even among these tough and hardy people, Joan was considered by her contemporaries to have been especially endowed with physical strength and stamina, courage, and a remarkable ability to recover from injury and illness.

9

A Century of Sorrows
The Royal Family

For someone born of royal blood, fate had dealt many disadvantages to Charles VII upon his birth. He was the eleventh child of Charles VI (1368–1422) and Isabeau of Bavaria (1371–1435), daughter of Stephen III, Duke of Bavaria. He should never have been king, but most of his siblings died before 1422, the year he became the Dauphin of France and heir to the throne:

1. Charles, the firstborn (b. 1386), lived only three months.

2. Jeanne (b. 1388) lived only until 1390.

3. Isabelle (b. 1389), who became the wife of the ill-fated Richard II of England, died in 1409 at the age of twenty.

4. Jeanne (b. 1391) died at forty-one in 1433.

5. Charles (b. 1392) lived for eight years until 1401.

6. Marie (b. 1393) died at forty-five as a nun in 1438.

7. Michelle (b. 1395) became the second wife of Philip the Good, Duke of Burgundy, a rival to Charles VII; she died in 1422 at age twenty-seven.

8. Louis (b. 1397) was eighteen at his death in 1415.

9. John (b. 1398) was the dauphin until he died in 1417, which opened the way for Charles VII to inherit the throne of France.

10. Catherine (b. 1401) became the wife of Henry V of England as part of the Treaty of Troyes, which disinherited Charles VII of his claim to the throne; she lived to see Charles VII recover much territory from the English, and died in 1437.

11. Charles VII (b. 1403), who, with the aid of Joan the Maiden, became King of France; he outlived all of his siblings and died in 1461 at age fifty-eight.

12. Philip (b. 1407) lasted only a matter of months; 1407 was also the year when John the Fearless, Duke of Burgundy, ordered the murder of his rival, Louis of Orléans, which precipitated the beginning of the French civil war.

The number and frequency of deaths in the royal family must have weighed heavily on the king and queen even in an age of high infant and child mortality, but their family's misfortunes did not end there. There was never a time when Charles VII knew his father to be without severe mental illness. Charles VI's first bouts of madness, now thought to be schizophrenia, occurred in 1392 when he killed four men during a military operation. During those intervals when he was too debilitated to rule, Philip the Bold, Duke of Burgundy ruled in his stead, but when Charles was mentally competent, he trusted in the counsel of Louis, Duke of Orléans. This intensified a political rivalry between the two great lords, each taking the opportunity to profit from the exemption of land taxes when power passed into his hands. The tension between them and their successors would eventually turn deadly and have disastrous consequences for France that lasted well into the reign of Charles VII.

Like her husband, Isabeau also suffered from mental illness. Although she never became insane, she experienced high levels of anxiety and had numerous phobias. Her physical health deteriorated when she contracted gout, and she eventually became so obese that she could hardly walk. She was notoriously promiscuous, which gave credence to her claim at the Treaty of Troyes in 1420 that Charles VII was illegitimate. She was also an avid contributor to the divisive partisan politics that resulted in civil war. When Charles was in his youth and being raised at the French court, Isabeau indulged him, but later in life she sided against him and allied herself with his rival, John the Fearless.

Civil war had reached within the royal family.

10

A Century of Sorrows
The Hundred Years' War (1413 to 1429)

In 1413, Henry V became King of England. Forceful, energetic, virile, and youthful, a gifted field commander and natural-born leader of men, Henry was determined to unite the people of England under his kingship and gain the throne of France, if not for himself, then for his successor. In 1415, the English under Henry landed in France. After a military expedition that inflicted great hardship on the people of Normandy, Henry defeated the French at Agincourt on October 25 in one of the most famous and important battles of the Middle Ages.

Large-scale pitched battles were rare in medieval times, but the fourteenth century saw a number of them that became legendary even if they were not decisive. The Battle of Agincourt hearkened back to previous battles when ordinary foot soldiers and bowmen were able to inflict a disastrous defeat on well-paid knights and highly prized lords:

- Flemish militias defeated a professional army of French knights at the Battle of Courtrai in 1302.

- Robert Bruce led a smaller Scottish force of pikemen and light horse and routed Edward II's larger English army at the Battle of Bannockburn in 1314.

- English longbowmen under Edward III decimated a much larger force of French mounted knights at the Battle of Crécy in 1346.

- The greatest English victory in the Hundred Years' War and one that caused great political turmoil in France was the Battle of Poitiers in 1356, at which English bowmen smashed unmounted French knights and captured the French king, John II (r. 1350–1364), and many other French nobles. John died in London in 1364 before his ransom could be paid.

Prior to the battle at Agincourt, however, it did not appear to either side that the English had a chance of replicating any of these famous victories. The French contingent was much larger, and many Englishmen were suffering from dysentery. On the night before the battle, the English were somber as they listened to the singing coming from the jubilant French camp, confident the next day would bring them a glorious victory and captured nobles to ransom. Henry walked among his dispirited troops encouraging them to regain their lost sense of hope.

To make matters worse, it rained heavily that night. Wet, ill, and exhausted, the English were at the end of a campaign of plunder and laden with booty that would be of no use to them in battle. It rained on the French as well, however, and more importantly it rained on the battlefield. If the weather favored anyone that night, it favored the English. Henry had one other critical advantage: four thousand longbowmen that accompanied his two thousand fighting men; and once again the English archers, as they had done in previous battles against the French, proved their inestimable worth on the medieval battlefield.

Bordered on both sides by wooded areas, the field was soft with wet grass and mud entirely unsuited for French knights in heavy armor and war horses protected by battle gear. Despite this severe disadvantage and in time-honored tradition, the French marched against the English longbowmen and, reminiscent of Crécy and Poitiers, were cut down in droves. Arrows darkened the sky as horses and men bogged down in mud, slipping and falling on top of one another. Unable to rise under the weight of their armor, men lay in heaps, some dead, some still living. Horses braying, men shouting, arrows flying. At one point the French seemed to be at the point of breaking the English line, and Henry, to his everlasting infamy and against all rules of chivalric warfare, ordered the murder of Frenchmen who had surrendered themselves as prisoners for ransom.

In the end, thousands of French bodies littered the field while the English dead numbered only a few hundred. Henry returned to England in triumphant celebration, hailed as a great king and renowned military commander. Agincourt was as lopsided a victory as Crécy and Poitiers. Among those captured was Charles, Duke of Orléans, whose half-brother, John of Orléans, would lead the defense of Orléans against a siege by the English in 1428–

1429 and later make vital contributions as a general in Charles VII's army. John of Orléans (made Count of Dunois in 1439) would become a compatriot of Joan and, as we shall later see, exercised great patience with her insistence on always taking the initiative in battle. In some ways, Joan resembled her countrymen, the over-confident French knights at Crécy, Poitiers, and Agincourt who plunged heedlessly into battle, but her relentless aggression stemmed from her faith in God and her voices and the belief that God would bring victory, rather than for the sake of chivalric honor and the hope of gaining noble hostages.

In 1416, Emperor Sigismund visited France and England in an attempt to make peace, but no progress was made and Henry invaded Normandy again in 1417. That year also saw the death of John, Dauphin of France,[10] leaving his brother Charles the title. After the Burgundians captured Paris in 1418, Charles fled the city and established his court at Bourges. His marriage to Marie of Anjou, daughter of Louis of Anjou, King of Naples, and Yolande of Aragon, put him firmly in the Armagnac camp.

Tensions between the Burgundians and the Armagnacs were somewhat alleviated when Charles attempted to reconcile with John the Fearless who had inherited the duchy when his father, Philip the Bold, passed away in 1404. At a second meeting in September 1419, however, John—who in 1407 ordered the slaying of Louis of Orléans, his uncle and Isabeau's lover—was

---

[10] Literally "dolphin," because the banner of the French heir included a dolphin.

killed from an axe blow to the head by one of the Armagnacs. Charles was present at the murder, but it is not certain if he knew of the assassination plot. He was nevertheless blamed vehemently by the Burgundians.

All of this helped precipitate the Treaty of Troyes. In revenge for the murder of John the Fearless,[11] the Burgundians helped Henry capture Paris along with King Charles VI. Henry was able to force his will on the enfeebled French monarch and obtained as his wife Charles' daughter, Catherine of Valois, who was Charles VII's older sister by two years. The treaty also stipulated that Henry and his successor by Catherine would be recognized as the rightful heir to the kingdom of France upon the death of Charles VI. The Treaty of Troyes was signed on May 21, 1420.

The Anglo-Burgundian alliance that resulted from this treaty cemented and formalized the ongoing French civil war. Isabeau was living under Burgundian protection and supported the treaty that disinherited Charles VII from the French throne. At the time of the signing, she hinted that he was illegitimate—thought by some to be the offspring of her lover, Louis of Orléans—and therefore not the rightful heir. The Burgundian alliance with the English and the insinuation of his illegitimacy by his mother were severe blows to Charles. For years afterward, many believed he could not rightfully inherit the throne "by the will of God" and be vested with the sacred power given only to lawful kings.

---

[11] Whose intrepidness may have cost him his life.

Fate intervened, however, and Henry died in 1422 at age thirty-five from dysentery contracted at the siege of Meaux. He was religious according to the standards of his day and was reading a book on the First Crusade shortly before he passed away. Henry had hoped to unite England and France in a crusade to the Holy Land, but his premature death put an end to this pious aspiration. Just two months later, Charles VI died and the throne of France became vacant.

Henry VI, the infant son of Henry V and Catherine, was recognized as king by the English and the Anglo-Burgundian party. Charles VII, at nineteen years old, was proclaimed king by the dauphinists with the justification that Charles VI was in no mental condition to agree to the terms specified in the Treaty of Troyes. The dauphinists who believed Charles VII to be illegitimate, supported Charles, Duke of Orléans, cousin of Charles VII, but he was still in England being held for ransom in comfortable confinement after having been captured at the Battle of Agincourt.

After Henry's death, small-scale fighting continued. Castles were besieged and villages, towns, and farms were raided. The English completed the conquest of Normandy at the Battle of Verneuil in 1424, and John of Lancaster, Duke of Bedford and brother of the deceased Henry V, ruled as regent for the boy-king Henry VI. Bedford, a capable albeit ill-tempered military commander, was determined to secure the kingdom of France for his nephew. Assisted by his alliance with Philip, Duke of

Burgundy, he consolidated his holdings in northern France and initiated a military campaign aimed at controlling the Loire River. For this to be successful, he needed to capture the fortified city of Orléans, which would open the way to Charles' main stronghold of Bourges. In 1428, the English under Bedford laid siege to Orléans.

Charles was in a seemingly impossible position. His treasury was nearly exhausted and his military forces were insufficient to expel the English from Guyenne and Normandy. Further, he was unable to consummate his claim to the throne, in no small part because Reims, the traditional city of French coronations, was in English hands. Supported by his mother-in-law, Yolande of Aragon, he waited apprehensively in what remained of his endangered territory south of the Loire River. He spent more than he could afford maintaining a court at the various castles still under his control. Short of a remarkable turn of events, it seemed only a matter of time until the English with Burgundian assistance would soon finish what remained of the conquest of France. There were times when he considered fleeing.

Joan's arrival on the scene in 1429 is somewhat of a historical oddity. The lifting of the siege at Orléans—in which she was instrumental, if not from a military standpoint, then from a spiritual and motivational one—marked a turning point in Charles' life and the Hundred Years' War that will forever be written into the pages of the history of Western Civilization.

Part Two

Mission of the Maiden

Consider your own calling, brothers. Not many of you were wise by human standards, not many were powerful, not many were of noble birth. Rather, God chose the foolish of the world to shame the wise, and God chose the weak of the world to shame the strong, and God chose the lowly and despised of the world, those who count for nothing, to reduce to nothing those who are something, so that no human being might boast before God.

1 Corinthians 1:26–29

11

A Hero Is Chosen
Birth and Early Years (1412 to 1428)

Much of France at the time of Joan's birth in 1412 was a land of ruined lives, dashed hopes, broken dreams, ravaged farms, and burned bridges. Then came the miracle of Joan, a Deus ex machina moment in the history of France and Western Europe that served as the catalyst for a series of setbacks to English power on the continent. The lifting of the siege of Orléans, in which she played a crucial part, turned the tide of the war and changed history. Her military career would be brief, lasting only about a year, but in that time she would be instrumental in the crowning of a French king and the loss of all of England's territorial possessions in France a mere twenty-two years after her death in 1431.

Few records were kept of peasant folk during medieval times, yet we know a great deal about Joan from the transcripts of her two trials. The first trial resulted in a condemnation for heresy, but in a remarkable turn of events (or perhaps a conspicuous instance of divine irony), her denouncement and defamation prompted a second trial that produced further documentation that led to her canonization in 1920.

Is it possible for one to give an adequate account of Joan's story without reference to the inscrutability of the divine will? A mere peasant girl from a small, unimportant village in the east of France, she was called by mysterious voices to a mission beyond her capacity to fulfill. She ended her life at age nineteen as one of the most famous women in Western history, hailed over the centuries as a symbol of French identity and nationalism, canonized by the Church who convicted and exonerated her, and who then cemented her triumph by naming her a patron saint of France. Could the explanation of such an unlikely sequence of events justly omit due recognition of the incomprehensible ways in which the Lord of History acts in the lives of his hero-saints? Could the rise of this Maiden owe more to any other cause than the workings of divine providence, and were not her voices truthful when they told her God would deliver her?

~

As we shall see, there is much in Joan's life that is remarkable, but there was little remarkable about her at her birth. Born in 1412, she was the second daughter and fourth child of Jacques d'Arc, a peasant farmer and minor official in Domrémy, and Isabelle, called Romée, who gave Joan all of the religious education she would receive. Both were illiterate, as was Joan.[12] The family home was located next to the village church, and the fact that it was made of stone and not wood, and that Jacques was able to raise five healthy children signifies that her father was a man of some social standing within his community who possessed at least modest wealth for a peasant.

Like other girls her age and social class, Joan learned to spin and sew, performed household chores, tended livestock, and worked in the garden and fields when needed, especially during harvest time. She was one of five children, having three brothers and a sister.[13] According to the transcripts of her trial of rehabilitation, she was an unusually pious girl, a trait she seems to have acquired from her mother, who had gone on pilgrimages and had a Dominican confessor. We also know that Joan's family was sociable, hard-working, and respected within their village community, and that Joan was articulate, intelligent, and popular. The moral and intellectual virtue Joan learned to practice at an early age would prove critical during her public mission and the last year of her life.

Domrémy was loyal to Charles VII and allied to the Armagnac cause, but it was located in the northeast of France, far from the dauphin's stronghold and isolated from any protection he or his

---

[12] Joan later learned to sign her name, and we have original letters dictated by her on which she affixed her signature.

[13] Jacquemin, Jean, and Pierre were older than Joan, but it is not known if she was older or younger than Catherine, who died before Joan began her public mission.

allies could give it. The civil war that began in 1407 had not reached Domrémy during Joan's childhood, although boys from her village would fight boys from Maxey, a village across the Meuse River that was aligned with Burgundy. Domrémy was in fact bordered on all sides by territory loyal to the Duke of Burgundy, and the ravages of war could not be staved off forever. It was only a matter of time before the serenity of Joan's early years would be shattered by the warfare characteristic of this era and locale.

Joan was three years old when Henry V defeated the French at Agincourt. In 1423, Robert de Saarbruck demanded protection money from the people of Domrémy, but this proved worthless when the village was attacked in 1425 by Burgundian marauders loyal to the King of England. Cattle were driven off, houses burned, and valuables stolen. Villagers reacquired some of their stolen property thanks to the generosity of a local lord and his knights who took up arms against the marauders, but the village church was burned and looted and many houses could only be repaired with great difficulty. Joan testified at her trial that this raid galvanized the citizens of Domrémy against the English, but she admitted that they loathed the Burgundians even more.

Joan was thirteen at the time of the attack, and shortly afterward she began to hear the voices of Saint Michael the Archangel, Saint Margaret (probably Margaret of Antioch), and Saint Catherine (probably Catherine of Alexandria). The first episode occurred while she was in her father's garden. She heard a voice accompanied by a bright light, which came from the direction of the church, a voice she identified as belonging to Saint Michael. The first revelations urged her to preserve her virginity for the sake of her salvation, and she was later told that she had been chosen by the "King of Heaven" to "bring reparation to the kingdom" of France. Joan remained faithful and for the most part obedient to these voices for the remainder of her life, as she believed they came to her by the will of God.

Joan's voices and their accompanying visions are a historical peculiarity and were remarkable at the time because of prophecies that were circulating throughout the French countryside of a "virgin" or "maiden" who would rise up and save France. Joan identified herself with these prophecies, thus acquiring for herself some authority and credibility, and especially at the siege of Orléans, she became known as the virgin who would save France. This was crucial to her self-image and identity. Joan was *the* "virgin" or "maiden"—"Jehanne la Pucelle," as she styled herself —who had come to drive the English out of France, and if necessary, by battle and bloodshed.

London

ENGLAND

English Channel

FLANDERS

HOLY
ROMAN
EMPIRE

Calais

Agincourt

Crécy

Rouen

Compiègne

NORMANDY

Reims

Vaucouleurs

Seine River

BRITTANY

Paris

Domrémy

ANJOU

Patay

Orléans

Loire River

Troyes

POITOU

Chinon

BURGUNDY

Nevers

1429

Poitiers

Bourges

AQUITAINE

DAUPHINÉ

Bordeaux

Garonne River

GUYENNE

ARMAGNAC

GASCONY

Toulouse

Avignon

LANGUEDOC

NAVARRE

Mediterranean
Sea

ARAGON

12

The Fullness of Time
Rise of the Maiden (1428 to 1429)

Joan continued to hear voices and see visions into 1428, although she told no one about them. Much of what was revealed by them pertained to her personally, and they especially emphasized her need to preserve her virginity. She was once pursued for marriage by a young man whose efforts she rebuffed, and she was aided by an ecclesial court that sided with her.

When she was sixteen, Joan's voices instructed her to go to Vaucouleurs, a nearby stronghold loyal to Charles VII. It was at this time that they began preparing her for her public mission of rescuing France from incessant warfare and crowning Charles VII King of France. The voices commanded her not to tell her parents of her intent to go to Vaucouleurs, so in May 1428 she obtained permission to stay at her cousin's home in a nearby town. Once there, she convinced her cousin's husband, Durand Laxart, to take her to Vaucouleurs.

When they arrived at Vaucouleurs, Joan immediately recognized, with help from her voices, the commander of the

Armagnac stronghold, Robert de Baudricourt, even though she had never seen him before. She boldly approached him and requested an armed escort to Chinon, where the itinerate court of the dauphin was staying. He bluntly refused. It was not uncommon at this time for girls or young women to believe they were on a divinely appointed mission to save France and then leave home to present themselves before important lords and ask for military assistance. Joan returned to Domrémy disappointed, but she left with her virginity intact, which could have been otherwise since Baudricourt was a notorious womanizer.

Domrémy was once again invaded by Burgundian marauders in July 1428, and Joan and her family were forced to flee with their fellow villagers to Neufchâtel. The English and Burgundians had recently begun a new campaign and they tried to take the fortress of Vaucouleurs but failed. A siege was also laid at Orléans, which came as very bad news to Charles and the Armagnacs.

While at Neufchâtel, Joan found employment at an inn, and in her free time she learned to ride a horse. This probably took place at the direction of her voices, as they continued to prepare her for her mission to relieve Orléans during the few weeks she stayed at Neufchâtel. She later testified at her trial that they told her she would last only a year or so, which helps to explain her characteristic impatience and determination to defeat the English and crown Charles king, as she must have felt great urgency to complete her divinely appointed task.

Without telling her parents, Joan returned to Vaucouleurs in January 1429. This time her persistence paid off, as the force of her personality and determined conviction won to her side some of Baudricourt's officers. Joan advised Baudricourt that the English were defeating the French in an important battle near Orléans, and days later a messenger arrived confirming her clairvoyance. He finally agreed to provide her with an armed escort in February for a journey to the dauphin through enemy-held territory. In anticipation of living among men in military service, Joan cut her hair short and began wearing men's clothing, probably for practical reasons and with a mind toward preserving her virginity. Along with the escort, Baudricourt gave her a horse and a sword.

Her second stay at Vaucouleurs until her departure for Chinon was a transformative moment for Joan, as if she had passed a significant milestone in life or an important rite of passage. From this moment on she referred to herself as "la Pucelle" as an allusion to the "maiden" who would save France. On February 13, she departed with her escort. Charles II, Duke of Lorraine, heard about Joan and asked that she visit him on the way to Chinon. The duke was ill and hoping for a cure. Joan proffered no cure, but she offered to pray for him and reproached him for his infidelity to his wife and for keeping a mistress. In return for her prayers and at her request, Charles permitted Joan to leave with his son, the Duke of Anjou, and other men who would be helpful to her. Along with these, she received a black horse and four francs.

After an eleven-day, 350-mile journey, Joan and her escort arrived at Fierbois near Chinon. She sent a messenger to the dauphin to request an audience and prayed at the chapel of Saint Catherine as she rested. Word had already spread throughout France about Joan the Maiden and her mission to save France, and the people of Chinon anticipated her arrival with great hope and curiosity.

Charles was reluctant to meet her and asked that she be examined first by clerics. A few days later, he agreed to her request for an interview but arranged to put her to a test. As she walked into the royal hall where he and his courtiers were gathered, her eyes searched the crowd for the dauphin, but Charles was dressed in clothes that did not distinguish him from the others. Never having seen him before, she immediately recognized him and presented herself before him. She hailed him as the King of France and told him of the mission she had received to raise the siege of Orléans and bring Charles to Reims to be anointed and crowned king.

A man in Charles' position could not be too trusting, though. After this brief introduction, he took Joan aside and spoke with her privately. We do not have a record of what was said, but when he rejoined the courtiers, he was in high spirits and was convinced enough to send her to Poitiers to be examined by theologians loyal to Charles. It was there that she predicted four future events, all of which came to pass:

1. The siege of Orléans would be lifted.

2. Charles VII would be consecrated and anointed King of France at Reims (which was still firmly under English control at this time).

3. Charles would regain the loyalty and obedience of Paris (which was firmly under Burgundian control).

4. Charles, Duke of Orléans, who was being held prisoner in England, would be set free and return to France.

Joan played a prominent role in the fulfillment of the first two predictions, and the other two were fulfilled after her death in 1431. The people of Paris returned their allegiance to Charles in 1437. Then in 1440, after twenty-five years in captivity and with the help of his former enemies, Philip the Good and Isabella of Portugal, Charles returned home to France a free man. He was forty-six years old at the time of his release, and it was said that he spoke English better than he did French.

The clerics at Poitiers found Joan to be a faithful Catholic and of virtuous moral character. They asked for a sign that she was from God and she said a sign would be provided at Orléans. No objections were raised against her participation in the relief of Orléans, and a recommendation was forwarded to Charles that her presence there might do some good. Further, it would provide a test for the authenticity of Joan's voices. After another examination by Charles' mother-in-law, Yolande of Aragon, to confirm her virginity, Joan was finally accepted as a member of Charles' army.

Charles had a special suit of armor made for her that weighed nearly sixty pounds. She still had the sword given to her by Baudricourt, but asked that a particular sword be fetched from behind the altar in the chapel of Saint Catherine at Fierbois, which her voices told her would be there. She described the sword as having five crosses on it and that it was buried either before or behind the altar. To their astonishment, those sent to retrieve the sword found it, easily rubbed off the rust, and brought it to her. She later broke it over the back of a camp prostitute, which alarmed Charles as an ill omen.

Joan was given permission to design her own standard which, according to John of Orléans, featured an image of Christ holding the fleur-de-lys. She reported at her trial that her voices had directed her with regard to its design and that she loved it more than any of her other military paraphernalia. Her banner became famous and she claimed that carrying it prevented her from ever killing anyone. Whether on a horse or on foot, it signaled to French troops her whereabouts on the battlefield[14] and at times served as a sort of rallying cry. It became a symbol of French resistance to the English, and much as the ancient Israelites

---

[14] We do not know what Joan looked like, but we have reports that she was short and sturdy, physically strong and healthy.

carried the Ark of the Covenant into battle, Joan's banner symbolized God's power in the midst of France's army.

Charles gave her a squire, John of Aulon, who was a member of his council, along with other fighting men and endowed her with some form of command, if only honorary. He also gave her a confessor, Jean Pasquerel, probably at her request, who was a mendicant friar and had met Joan's mother on pilgrimage. To complete her retinue, she was joined by her brothers Jean and Pierre, who were also given suits of armor.

The men who served with her were loyal and enthusiastic. They viewed her as the prophesied maiden sent by God and their best hope for preventing almost certain defeat by the English. She had never been in a battle, never studied to be a knight or learned military strategy, and never traveled far from her home village until recently, but she had qualities that could not be taught. She was charismatic, had a warrior spirit, and possessed extraordinary physical and mental stamina. She was highly intelligent and had an outstanding memory, which enabled her to give sharp responses useful for gaining the respect of men. She also had firm convictions of the righteousness of her cause and was confident in the divine support she expected to receive.

In short, her faith was unshakable.

A Hero Is Chosen

13

Joan's Hero-Event
The Maiden Arrives

Joan joined a group of reinforcements at Blois in late April 1429 before departing with them for Orléans. The dire predicament of the Armagnacs was not entirely hopeless, but the English had the city almost entirely surrounded, even if some of the fortifications were weak. Resistance within the city had not yet been broken, and the citizens of Orléans had appealed to Philip, Duke of Burgundy, for clemency since its lord, Louis, Duke of Orléans, was a prisoner in England. He would gladly have taken possession of the city in return for its neutrality, but Bedford rejected the deal. Although he gave no military assistance in resisting the siege, Philip withdrew a small detachment of Burgundian soldiers who were fighting alongside the English.

Joan's entrance onto the scene acted as an immediate catalyst to French morale. Forceful and commanding, a dynamo for the dauphinist cause, she showed impatience with any strategy that involved anything less than a direct, frontal assault. Her inclination was always to charge, and the commands she issued were never ambiguous. She had only a year to complete her divinely appointed mission and believed it could only fail through inaction or treachery. The letters Joan dictated to the Duke of Bedford were imbued with religious language that defined her cause as far beyond a merely political or military one. She was fighting under God's command and would receive his power, and if Bedford and the English refused to yield, they would succumb to the power of her sword.

Joan arrived at Orléans and officially joined the Armagnac army on April 29, 1429. Charles' forces were led by John of Orléans, who a few days earlier had taken the unusual step of traveling to greet her at Blois in person. Despite his misgivings about the authenticity of this prefigured maiden, he welcomed her into his camp. Throughout the course of her service in the French army, Joan frequently tested the patience of French commanders and strategists with her insistence on always being on the attack, yet John of Orléans consistently treated her with respect and her cause with great deference, even if he never gave her much of a role in commanding the army.

Yet Joan's real power lay in her influence over the troops, whose favor she had won. The odds were entirely against a late-teenage peasant woman establishing genuine comradery with battle-hardened medieval men-at-arms, but she was able to gain their respect through the force of her conviction in the divine origin of her cause and overcame the liability of her gender so thoroughly that soldiers who served with her reported that they never felt carnal lust for her, even if some of them had seen her breasts while she was dressing. They were captivated by her virginity, believing it gave her divine power that could be channeled toward success in combat. She insisted that the troops stop swearing, that they confess their sins and attend Mass, and that they refrain from pillaging and looting civilians. She was not only "la Pucelle," the incarnation of a prophecy that promised deliverance from endless war, but something resembling a living saint.

Volunteers flocked to her banner, and many obeyed her in the midst of battle when she ordered an attack. The Middle Ages has often been called an "age of faith"—faith in God, in the Church, in miracles, and in prophecies—and it seemed that all of France, at least those who remained loyal to the dauphin, had now put their faith in "Jehanne la Pucelle."

Her first assignment was to help transport food into Orléans for its beleaguered inhabitants, an assignment she did not at first accept with great alacrity. Had Joan's relationship with John of Orléans been based on their initial encounters and had John been less of a gentleman, it would have been a difficult relationship indeed. Joan expected that the Armagnacs would immediately attack the English upon her arrival and that God would bring victory to the French through her active leadership. She interpreted her assignment to food transportation as John's attempt to deceive her and greeted him at their next meeting with sharp words. John was sympathetic and courteously explained that reinforcements were needed before an attack could be successful, and that there was more to warfare than combat. Joan, abstemious by nature, balked at such a mundane task which she viewed as deviating from her mission, but agreed to assist nonetheless. There was still the problem that the contrary winds were preventing the supply ships from sailing downstream to the city, but Joan told John not to worry, and at that moment the direction of the wind changed. John was astounded but Joan seemed unsurprised.

The English were unable to prevent the transport ships from reaching the city, and the thirty thousand citizens of Orléans received the necessary provisions. Aside from supplying them with food, John considered their morale and asked Joan to accompany him into the city. She demurred—another delay to a direct military confrontation with the English—but once again yielded to John's request.

Although Joan was given no authority to command within the French army, her role as a spiritual figurehead and morale boost was of inestimable value and precisely what the Armagnacs needed at this moment. Any success to which she could be linked would only confirm her identity as "la Pucelle" sent by God to drive out the English and crown Charles king. Riding alongside John in plain sight of the English, who did not have enough soldiers to secure the entire perimeter, she entered the city seated on a white palfrey. The populace came out to greet her with great rejoicing. The Maiden had arrived and had a year to complete her mission, yet she would only need to wait a matter of days before her first grand (and historic) success would be achieved. Within ten days, the English would lift the siege and be in full retreat.

14

The Tide of History Turns
The Battle of Orléans

The city of Orléans had been under siege since October 1428. As the Armagnac army awaited reinforcements, Joan dictated letters to Bedford and other English captains. The first two letters have not survived. A third letter, dated March 22, 1429, was sent over the walls of the English fortifications on the tip of an arrow to the jeers of onlooking English soldiers who derisively called her a "cowgirl" and "whore" and told her to go back to her village and "tend to her cows." In this letter (which probably included similar content to the two lost letters), Joan demanded that the English abandon their fortified positions around the city and surrender to "the Maiden...sent here by God, King of Heaven." She also required that they return all of the cities they had taken and pay for all the damage they had caused to the people of France. She promised to have mercy and make peace if they obeyed her demands and added that they could "come to join her company." Those who refused, she threatened to have killed. Bedford responded with silence.

Joan viewed herself in the service of the "King of Heaven" more than the French king, and this more than anything else gave her confidence. Yet there were a number of instances, including the moments leading up to the Battle of Orléans, when this confidence bordered on impertinence. She first demonstrated her characteristic boldness when she petitioned Baudricourt for an armed escort to meet the dauphin, and later spoke audaciously to John of Orléans when she felt cheated at having been assigned to food transport instead of combat duty. Further on in this story, when John Fastolf was leading a new English army to Orléans, Joan threatened to behead John if he failed to notify her of his arrival. Yet one person's rashness and impetuosity is another's self-confidence and decisiveness, and in a different age and under dire circumstances, the line between the two can become blurred.

Episodes like these may be understood as a sign of Joan's faith in the divine origin of her mission and the trust she placed in her voices. The villagers who testified at her trial of rehabilitation described her as polite and well-spoken when she lived among them, and it is probable that she realized that, as a young teenage peasant girl, she needed to be forceful to be heard by men in a world of battlefields, armament, siege engines, and conquest. She was adapting to the unfamiliar as best she could, and like other young women in their late teens, she was not yet fully mature.

This process of adjustment to a medieval military way of life was not without its misjudgments and growing pains, and we must be careful about imposing our modern stained-glass notions of sanctity upon this rough and rugged, tough, talented, and intelligent girl of peasant stock. It is true that she could be unreasonable, demanding, and combative, but she was also an uncompromising visionary and idealist, an ardent young woman overcompensating for her youthfulness and femininity with seemingly haughty threats that sometimes ended in fits of frustration and tears.

Having failed to persuade the English to surrender, Joan returned to camp to await John of Orléans' orders. He was still recovering from a wound received in February 1429 during the "Day of the Herrings" when French forces failed to defeat a small English detachment carrying supplies—much of it pickled herring that would be eaten during Lent. Responsibility for the disaster fell upon John Stuart of Darnley, a Scotsman, who impetuously charged without waiting for reinforcements and paid for this indiscretion with his life. Other important commanders lost that day included Louis of Rochechouart and William of Albret. The debacle at the "Battle of the Herrings" further depressed the morale of the Armagnac soldiers and the citizens of Orléans, and confidence in John as commander of the French army, even if he later proved to be a capable strategist and field commander, diminished in its aftermath.

On Wednesday, May 4, Joan dined with John and learned from him that an English army commanded by John Fastolf was approaching. This delighted her and she insisted that John send word to her of Fastolf's arrival or, "I will have your head cut off!"

In his characteristic tactfulness, John assured her that he would send word to her and that he believed she would make good on her promise if he did not. When dinner was over, Joan went to her quarters to rest.

Despite his courteousness, John and the other French officers did not consider Joan much more than a mascot or good luck charm, perhaps useful for morale and inspiration but not for devising strategy and commanding troops in battle. That same day while Joan was asleep, John led a contingent of troops against the English-occupied monastery of Saint-Loup. Joan awoke suddenly with a warning from her voices that French blood was being spilled. She chided her page, Louis of Courtes, and demanded to be armed and her horse readied for battle. As she was about to gallop off toward the Burgundy Gate, her standard was passed to her through a window.

Joan assumed she was going into battle against Fastolf's army and was surprised to find that Saint-Loup was only a small skirmish. The attacking French were faltering but gave a great shout when Joan arrived, and as it would for the entire Hundred Years' War, her appearance turned the tide of battle. Joan rallied a group of soldiers and led a charge that invigorated the entire French contingent. The English were assaulted with such ferocity that they were forced to abandon the monastery, and in order to save their lives, they dressed in church vestments. Joan, believing them to be priests or monks, halted the attack.

Saint-Loup was more than a moral victory for the French as it provided the strategic advantage of allowing access to a second gate through which the French could resupply the citizens of Orléans and a base from which they could conduct further sallies. Saint-Loup was also Joan's first battle. Her previous exposure to war was limited to the military brigands who raided Domrémy, and she was not prepared for the bloodshed of a battlefield. Her confessor and page reported that she was highly distraught and wept for those she believed had died without receiving sacramental confession. She ordered her troops to confess their sins and give thanks to God for the victory.

The following day was the Feast of the Ascension, and it was the custom according to what remained of the chivalric code to abstain from battle on holy days, so Joan refused to fight. She instead confessed her sins and received the Eucharist, to which she had a great devotion. She also sent three letters to the English reiterating her demands, but they did not respond and prevented two of her messengers from returning.

Against the wishes of the governor of the city, Raoul of Gaucourt, and the high command of the French army, Joan led a group of men on a sortie on Friday, May 6. She crossed the Loire River and attempted to attack a bastille called Saint-Jean-le-Blanc, but the English retreated to the monastery-turned-fort of Saint-Augustin south of a bridge called the Tourelles. The French officers wanted to stop the advance for the day, but as their soldiers were returning to their bases, the English attacked. Joan and Étienne of Vignolles, known as La Hire, turned to meet the attackers and were joined by a large group of soldiers. The battle proved so successful that the French dislodged the English from Saint-Augustin and forced them to withdraw to the Tourelles.

Satisfied with these unanticipated victories, members of the French high command wanted to consolidate their gains and wait for reinforcements, but Joan insisted on battle. She received a wound in her foot from a spiked ball and predicted she would be wounded again the next day. As anticipated, an arrow pierced her shoulder as she was leading an attack against the Tourelles, and she was briefly removed from the battlefield to receive medical attention. It was suggested that a charm be applied to the wound, but she refused saying she would rather be dead than do something against the will of God. After it was dressed with fat, Joan returned to battle.

As evening approached, John of Orléans sought to retire, but Joan insisted that victory was at hand. He permitted the attack to continue while Joan went to a vineyard to pray. When she returned fifteen minutes later carrying her standard, the French soldiers cheered and the attack was renewed in earnest. A trumpet was blown to retreat but Joan ignored it. Citizens from inside the city aided the French men-at-arms by temporarily repairing the broken bridge with ladders and boards and attacking the Tourelles from the rear. The English, suspecting sorcery from Joan, lost heart. Their defenses broke and the French men-at-arms swarmed over the walls.

Earlier that day, the French had sailed a large boat filled with wood and a flammable substance under the bridge. As the English withdrew, the boat was set ablaze and the bridge collapsed, killing over four hundred English soldiers who drowned under the weight of their armor. Among them was their commander, William Glasdale, whom Joan called "Classidas." She wept for the man she had previously threatened and for the souls of the English dead, but the Tourelles, which had been occupied by the English since last October, was now liberated. The people of Orléans rejoiced and Joan accompanied John as he reentered the city. Joan was given further medical attention for her wound later that evening.

On Sunday, May 8, the English abandoned the remainder of their fortifications and arrayed themselves in battle formation expecting the French to oppose a full-scale retreat. Joan was riding her white stallion and carrying her banner as she accompanied a large force of soldiers to meet the English. She forbade them to attack in respect for the chivalric rules of warfare, however. This caused great consternation among the French men-at-arms who, according to a contemporary account, were vexed and displeased with having to obey this command. Joan had two Masses said in the field. The battle lines were positioned close together. She permitted the French to defend themselves if attacked, but the English declined battle. They were convinced that Joan was a witch and had defeated them through the power of the devil. After an hour, the English departed by a road that led away from Orléans and retreated toward Jargeau.

There would be no Crécy, Poitiers, or Agincourt on this day. The English retreated in defeat, and French victory at the Battle of Orléans was sealed. We may only wonder in hindsight what harm the French might have inflicted on young Henry VI's claim to the French crown had Joan allowed the French to attack their demoralized and bewitched opponent. The rules of warfare were changing rapidly, however, and on a later occasion Joan would not observe such chivalric niceties, an omission that would be used against her during her trial for heresy.

A novena of days had passed since Joan the Maiden joined the Armagnac army at Orléans on April 29. In this short span of time, the siege had been lifted and the English campaign that had once threatened to extinguish the dauphinist cause had been blunted. When the clerics who interviewed Joan at Poitiers asked for a sign, she told them it would be given to them at Orléans.

She had delivered on that promise.

15

Mission and Task
The Loire Campaign

Joan had accomplished an important part of her mission at Orléans and her star was rising. Morale in the Armagnac army was high, and despite disregarding orders, she had earned some credibility with the French captains, especially John of Orléans and the twenty-five-year-old John II, Duke of Alençon. Joan insisted that Charles be brought to Reims to be crowned without delay, since French kings had been crowned there for almost a thousand years and most citizens of France would not accept the legitimacy of a king unless the coronation took place in Reims. It was also vital that the legitimate heir be anointed with the sacred oil that was, according to legend, used in 496 to baptize Clovis, first king of the Franks, and then to anoint his successors.

The theory prevalent at this time was that kings possessed a divine right to rule, but God's blessing came only through lawful coronation and sacramental anointing with sacred oils; for the French, this meant oil from the ancient vial kept at Reims. Inducing the city to submit to Charles was crucial, and his crowning there would unite much of France behind him. It might even help to persuade the Burgundians to lay aside old grievances and abandon their alliance with the English.

A march through enemy territory would be dangerous, however, and the city had not yet pledged its allegiance to Charles. The French would first need to secure strongholds along the Loire River and drive the English northward before a coronation at Reims could take place. With any luck, the Burgundian garrison guarding the city would withdraw and its citizens be persuaded to join Charles without the need to besiege or attack it.

The royal army finally departed from Orléans on May 9, but the Loire Campaign did not begin until June 11. Sometime after May 23, Joan visited the Duke and Duchess of Alençon. The duke's father, John I, had been killed at the Battle of Agincourt in 1415, and Henry V gave the duchy to the Duke of Bedford. John I was succeeded by his son Pierre, who died in 1425, which opened the way for John II (1407–1476) to inherit the duchy if the English could be expelled.

An heir without an estate, John II was entrusted by his mother to Charles the dauphin but was captured by the English at the Battle of Verneuil on August 6, 1424, when he was only fifteen years old. Held prisoner by the Duke of Clarence, his ransom was finally paid on February 21, 1429, when his wife sold her jewels and he agreed to surrender other fiefs in France. French victory at the Battle of Orléans was a great blessing for the titular duke, however, as he soon recovered these fiefs and was eventually able to regain possession of the duchy of Alençon in 1449.

John II first heard about Joan when she arrived at Chinon to meet Charles for the first time. He quickly departed from a hunting excursion and hurried there to meet her. Joan was fascinated with Alençon and the two became friends. When she visited him and the duchess before the commencement of the Loire Campaign, Joan asked Alençon to join her in her quest to drive the English out of France. The duchess protested, but after assurances from Joan that she would return him safely, she consented.

Charles appointed Alençon to command the Armagnac army during the Loire Campaign and Joan served as his trusted advisor. The first town to be taken was Jargeau, which the French attacked on June 12. At one point during the battle, Joan told Alençon, whom she called her "fair duke," to move from the place he was standing because a projectile was about to land there. Another man named du Lude stepped into that place a few moments later and was struck and killed. Shortly afterward, Joan was climbing a siege ladder with her standard in hand and was struck by a rock that cracked her helmet. At the end of the battle, 1,100 Englishmen lay dead and Jargeau returned to the dauphinist cause.

The French then marched on Meung, gaining control of the south bank of the river on June 15. Beaugency was besieged on June 16, and the English garrison was forced to retreat into the central stronghold. Alençon learned that Fastolf and John Talbot, first Earl of Shrewsbury, were each leading armies toward Beaugency, so he offered the garrison safe passage if they would surrender the fortress. They accepted and withdrew before the English army could arrive.

It was during the Loire Campaign that Joan was approached by Arthur of Richemont, Constable of France, who wished to rejoin the Armagnac cause. His loyalty was questioned by many in the dauphinist camp because he briefly sided with the English, and Charles and his advisor, Georges de La Trémoïlle, refused his offer. Joan, however, seeing an opportunity to strengthen her forces, admitted him. This was another example of how Joan was willing to disregard the will of her superiors if it served her cause. We can only wonder how Joan's insubordination was viewed by Charles and his advisors, and if this view did not affect the counsel he received after Joan had been captured by the Burgundians and might still have been ransomed. But then we would not have the Joan we have today.

During the siege of Beaugency, Fastolf marched at the head of an army to join forces with Talbot so that together they might relieve its garrison, but once he learned that it surrendered, he realized that the French campaign could not be stopped and withdrew toward Paris. This presented an opportunity and Joan pressed Alençon to attack. What followed was the Battle of Patay where the French caught up with the retreating English on June 18 and destroyed them. La Hire played a prominent role when he attacked and routed a surprised English contingent. Fastolf fled amidst the confusion and his troops were thrown into disarray. Talbot remained to fight, but he was captured and taken prisoner. According to a Burgundian chronicler, the English lost around two thousand men, which represented a substantial portion of their continental army. The French, miraculously, lost only three.

Joan arrived late on the battlefield and did not take part in the slaughter. She witnessed the aftermath of victory when La Hire and the French brutally murdered many of the English who surrendered, keeping alive only two hundred wealthy nobles as prisoners for ransom. At one point she witnessed a French soldier mortally wound an Englishman on the head. Climbing from her horse, she cradled him in her arms and heard his last confession. Whatever Joan thought of her enemies prior to battle and despite her bravado, once she laid eyes on the vanquished foe, she on more than one occasion wept copiously for their souls and showed sincere concern for their salvation.

The Loire Campaign was brief and conclusive. Not only had the French recaptured strategic bases on the Loire, they had also crippled English and Burgundian forces to the extent that there were not enough fighting men to defend northern France from invasion. This opened the way for a march to Reims and Charles' coronation. The recent turn of events must also have given the Burgundians pause for thought. If a legitimate French king were crowned and if the English no longer had the manpower to defeat the Armagnacs, then perhaps some reasonable accommodation could be made with Charles to end the civil war.

16

Mission and Task
The March to Reims and the Crowning of a King

The news of the recent spate of French victories spread throughout Europe. Joan became famous overnight and was given much credit for France's reversal of fortune. The tale grew in the telling and her contributions were exaggerated. She would not live past the age of nineteen, but she had already become a living legend.

After the bloodshed at Patay, John of Orléans rode with Joan to meet the dauphin. Charles was in good spirits and the discussion between him and his advisors about strategy revolved around two options. The first was to march north into Normandy and reconquer lost lands and, if it seemed propitious, to march toward Paris. A majority of the captains and royal counselors advocated this option. The second, advocated by Joan, was to march to Reims without delay and have Charles anointed and crowned king. She argued that once Charles was endowed with the sacred right to rule, he would be accepted by the people.

Subduing Normandy was clearly the wisest strategic alternative, although the royal counselors acknowledged the political advantages a march to Reims promised if successful. Joan insisted she was being led by her voices but met determined opposition from the royal counselors. She resorted to prayer, and her confidence was soon renewed. Charles hesitated but was eventually won over by Joan's importunity.

On June 29, the French army marched to Reims from Gien with Joan riding at Charles' side. Letters were written to a number of towns and cities along the way announcing the dauphin's approach, promising pardon, and encouraging their loyalty. Letters were written to the Duke of Burgundy urging reconciliation. The English did not oppose the march, and after brief periods of negotiation the towns and cities along the army's route pledged obedience to Charles and provided his army with food. A garrison of English and Burgundian soldiers remained at Troyes, where the treaty had been signed in 1420 that disinherited Charles from the throne. They refused to surrender, but Joan ordered that the moat be filled with wood and had cannon placed within firing range of the city walls. They soon capitulated and Charles entered Troyes on Sunday, July 10.

As the army approached Reims, a delegation from the city came out to meet Charles on July 16 and offered their full obedience. The Burgundian garrison fled. Pierre Cauchon, the Bishop of Beauvais and former rector of the University of Paris, still loyal to the Anglo-Burgundian cause, departed the city. He had helped negotiate the Treaty of Troyes in May 1420 that disinherited Charles and would later preside over the trial that condemned Joan. That same day, Charles made a triumphant entry into Reims with Joan riding at his side.

The consecration ceremony took place the following day, Sunday, July 17, on the altar of the cathedral at Reims. Four knights accompanied by many high-ranking Church officials carried the sacred vial in procession from Saint-Rémy Abbey to the cathedral. As was the custom, the king took an oath of loyalty and prostrated himself beside the archbishop while the *Te Deum* was sung and litanies were chanted. The highlight of the ceremony was the sacramental anointing by the archbishop, who mixed a drop of oil from the sacred vial with Holy Chrism. The king was then vested with ring, scepter, spurs, and royal garments, and the royal crown was placed on his head. The archbishop and important nobles then paid homage. Joan, dressed in armor and carrying her standard, knelt before him, embraced his legs, and hailed him as the true king by the will of God. Charles was no longer the dauphin; he was Charles VII, King of France.

After the ceremony, Joan dictated a letter to the Duke of Burgundy pressing him to make peace with France's new king. She spoke on behalf of the "King of Heaven," urging Philip to mutual pardon and reconciliation with Charles. She entreated him to withdraw his troops from northern France, and if he refused, she asserted, he would be waging war against the King of Heaven as well as the rightful King of France. There would be great bloodshed, she declared, against his soldiers and all who "war against us." She did not consult with Charles or his advisors before sending this letter, however, nor was she privy to the discussions that were taking place between the Armagnacs and the Burgundians. The Duke of Burgundy was dealing deceitfully with Charles and his advisors, and the king naively agreed to a fifteen-day truce.

17

Winds of Change
Joan's True Vocation

From the moment Joan put her feet on the path that permanently led her away from Domrémy, the trajectory of her life course rose precipitously until she reached the pinnacle of French society.[15] It had taken five months to crown Charles VII, and five months after his coronation in December 1429, Charles would raise her and her family to the status of nobility. She was famous throughout Europe and had made her permanent mark on history, but fame and success did not matter much to Joan. What motivated her more than anything else was her mission and fulfilling the will of God as manifested to her through her voices.

Following Charles' coronation, Joan wondered aloud to John of Orléans if she should go home to Domrémy and resume the pastoral life of a peasant. Three reasons leap forth to explain why she would consider this option: First, she was dissatisfied with the

---

[15] Except for Baudricourt's refusal of her first request in May 1428 and beginning with his consent at her second visit to send her to Chinon with an armed escort.

policy of the king and his advisors toward the Burgundians and realized that her aggressive style of warfare was incompatible with the royal council's preference for diplomacy. Second, she may have been homesick (not unusual for someone her age, gender, and life experience). And third, she might have considered her mission fulfilled, at least those parts that were within her power to accomplish. Her sudden and unexpected arrival breathed new hope into the demoralized royal army. She had played an indispensable part in the victory at Orléans and in the Loire Campaign. The dauphin she sought to crown was now king. Even if the third and fourth predictions she made at Poitiers remained unfulfilled, she had completed the substance of her mission in dazzling swiftness that left little doubt except to her enemies about the divine origin of her voices.

Yet Joan did not return home, and we may reasonably assume that the king would have granted this favor had she requested it. So why did she stay? What precisely was the mission given to her by her voices? Were the predictions she made at Poitiers part of that mission? Was she certain of what God was asking of her?

When she met the dauphin for the first time at Chinon, she announced to him what was in effect a summary of her mission. She told him she would only last a year and that she had come to:

1. Drive out the English
2. Bring him to Reims to be crowned king
3. Free Charles, Duke of Orléans, from captivity in England
4. Raise the siege of Orléans.

The predictions she made to the clerics at Poitiers coincide with the above, but not precisely. She prophesied that:

A. The English would be driven away and the siege of Orléans would be lifted (1,4 above)

B. Charles VII would be crowned king at Reims (2)

C. Paris would become loyal again to Charles

D. Charles, Duke of Orléans, would be freed and return to France (3).

To "drive out the English" (1, A) is the only item on either list that is ambiguous. It could mean to "relieve the siege of Orléans and drive them from Armagnac territory." If so, then she fulfilled this element of her mission at the completion of the Loire Campaign, which was in hindsight the beginning of the end for the English in the Hundred Years' War. The English had not only been driven out of Charles' stronghold, but they could no longer defend their territory in northern France.

To "drive out the English" could also mean to "expel them entirely from France."[16] This interpretation is also possible with regard to Joan and her mission, but she knew she would last only a year, and assuming that God does not ask the impossible, to expel the English entirely from France within a year with a cautious king and hesitant royal council would have been most unlikely for Joan to accomplish. Given the circumstances, it is doubtful that this was a part of her divinely appointed mission, at

---

[16] A long process that was not completed until 1453.

least during her time on earth.[17] Perhaps she mused on the idea of returning to Domrémy because she recognized the improbability of such a feat and wondered if God would be satisfied with her obedience up to that point.

With regard to Paris' allegiance to Charles (C), she did not announce to him at Chinon that she was sent to secure the loyalty of Paris, a prediction she had made at Poitiers. It is not likely that she believed this to be a part of her mission either, since she knew she would only last a year and predicted that Paris would return to Charles within seven years.[18] It is possible that she may have at some later point conflated the predictions of Poitiers with the mission given to her by her voices and included the liberation of Paris as part of her mission.[19] Or perhaps she did not conceive of the recovery of Paris as a constituent part of her mission, but understood it to be at least congruent with her mission even if it was not explicitly required of her by her voices.

Finally, with regard to liberating the Duke of Orléans (3), she announced to Charles at Chinon that she had been sent (mission) to free the duke from captivity, but it is not likely she believed after the coronation at Reims that she had the power to accomplish this given the dispositions of the king and his royal

---

[17] Her mission may have continued into eternity and she may have had something to do with the eventual outcome.

[18] Paris pledged fealty to Charles in 1436 and he entered the city in 1437. This fulfilled Joan's prophecy that it would occur within seven years.

[19] The attack in September 1429, in which Joan took part, failed.

council.[20] Therefore, she may have considered it impossible for her to drive the English out of France and to rescue the Duke of Orléans, and since God does not ask the impossible, this realization may have given rise to her expressed desire to return to Domrémy.

~

There is a general consensus among historians that the greatest captains of warfare in history are:

1. Alexander the Great of Macedon

2. Julius Caesar of Rome

3. Hannibal of Carthage

4. Genghis Khan of the Mongols

5. Gustavus Adolphus of Sweden

6. Frederick the Great of Prussia

7. Napoleon Bonaparte of France.

Had Joan returned to Domrémy after Charles' crowning at Reims, or had she stayed with the army and taken a more passive role by deferring to the royal advisors who consistently advised caution and diplomacy, she would certainly not have made this list, but she would have been remembered as an unexpectedly successful captain of warfare, even if she did not have overall command of the French army. If that were the case, we would not

---

[20] Charles of Orléans was finally freed in November 1440 after twenty-five years in captivity and nine years after Joan's death, but only with the help of Philip, Duke of Burgundy, with whom Joan was at war.

have the Joan we have today and we probably would not have the transcripts from her trials, which give us more information about her than any other woman in history up to Queen Elizabeth I of England and Mary, Queen of Scots.

But there is another possible course history might have taken: Had circumstances been different and had Joan accomplished all that she announced at Chinon, including the expulsion of the English from France, and all that she predicted at Poitiers, then historians might very well rank her among the greatest captains of warfare. Yet beyond the speculation of historians and the complexities of this current temporal age, there remains one final possibility: that Joan was able to accomplish with divine assistance the whole of her mission and fulfill all four predictions posthumously as a saint in heaven. God does not ask the impossible, but all things are possible with God (Matthew 19:26).

~

She may have considered returning to Domrémy and the pastoral life of her youth, which was slipping away from her on the battlefields of central France and in the geopolitical events of her day, but the truth is that the path to Domrémy was forever closed to her and perhaps she realized it. Had she returned, she probably would have been hunted down by the Burgundians or the English, or perhaps some enterprising bounty hunter who would make a substantial profit by selling her to her enemies.

Joan must have sensed the winds of change blowing after Reims. Her voices had told her she would last only a year, "perhaps a little longer." If she knew that her mission entailed the sacrifice of her life, she did not say. Judging from her comportment at her trial, and especially in her expectation of being delivered by God and the horror she displayed at being convicted of heresy, it seems she did not assume that her mission would necessarily end in death.

The winds of change were in truth blowing in Joan's life, even if she did not know where they would lead her. The stunning successes of the first five months gave way to mixed military results after Reims. She would be no Caesar on the battlefields of France, no Napoleon come to defend her honor. Joan was a warrior but not a soldier who, above all else, is obliged to obey. Nor did she demonstrate the prudential judgment of a trained military officer. Had she been reared in the martial arts of her day or attended a military academy, which would one day become the norm in Europe, perhaps these qualities might have been instilled in her. But the opportunity to make soldiery a profession was not afforded to Joan, nor did her mission call for it, and nor did her gender and station in life as a peasant permit it.

Joan is not remembered as a great captain of warfare but as a warrior, a prodigy, a phenomenon. Her success did not depend on prescient military strategy, but on courage, fortitude, a single-minded determination and unwavering conviction that she was given a divinely inspired mission, and an unrelenting dynamism that contrasted sharply with her unsure and wary king. Her sense was always to press forward, to charge, because she knew she had only a year. In the end, she laid down her life for the two kings she served, defending the honor of one at the sermon preached before her execution, and calling out the name of the other as the fire licked up and eventually consumed her, all the while trusting in her voices and the God who had led her to the pyre.

Joan is not remembered as a great captain of warfare but as a virgin, hero, martyr, and saint—which was in fact her true vocation. The historian and moralist may comb through her story and find defects and gaffes, but no hero is faultless except Jesus of Nazareth and no saint perfect except Mary of Nazareth. Not all heroes are saints, and not all saints are heroes. Despite her faults of temperament and youth, Joan was both.

18

Turning Point
Defeat at Paris

The Duke of Bedford was now regrouping his forces after the defeat at Orléans and disaster at Patay. A unit raised by his uncle, Cardinal Henry Beaufort, Bishop of Winchester, that was supposed to march to Bohemia under papal authorization to fight the Hussites was diverted to France to make up for the losses. They arrived in Calais and on July 15 were immediately redirected to Paris to reinforce the Burgundian garrison.

The Burgundians were simultaneously negotiating with the English to maintain their alliance and raise a new army, and in bad faith parleying with the Armagnacs, promising to cede possession of Paris as a precursor to a permanent peace agreement. Georges de La Trémoïlle was the lead negotiator on behalf of the French. Along with Charles' mother-in-law, Yolanda of Aragon, Queen of Anjou and Sicily, La Trémoïlle was one of Charles' top advisors and most important financiers. He was also of the faction that consistently advocated patience and diplomacy rather than the financially crippling armed conflict that Joan unfailingly encouraged. Negotiations between the Burgundians and Armagnacs produced a deceptively fruitful fifteen-day truce.

Charles might have seized the initiative after Reims as his recent string of victories had the Anglo-Burgundian alliance on its heels. He could count on Joan's miraculous ability to galvanize the army with the divine approbation that seemed to accompany her. He was also fortunate to have a number of reliable officers (e.g., John of Orléans, La Hire, the Duke of Alençon), and his army (which he could not afford to pay) had swelled with men and enthusiasm. Had he possessed the disposition of a man like Henry V, the choice would have been reflexive and the war might have ended sooner. In any case, it ended in France's favor and while Charles was still king.

But there were other considerations. Charles may have been plagued by guilt for the murder of John the Fearless in September 1419, and his severe financial limitations were surely a part of his decision. Perhaps with this in mind, he heeded the advice of La Trémoïlle and directed his efforts toward diplomacy. The fifteen-day truce was a mirage, however, and peace between Burgundy and the Armagnacs was not finally realized until the Treaty of Arras was signed in 1435.

From this point on, Charles and Joan were on divergent paths. Charles' road led to a diplomatic peace with Burgundy, Joan's to decisive military confrontation that resulted in immediate victory. The two paths could not be reconciled.

Joan was not alone in her judgment, as Alençon also believed that Paris should be attacked without delay. Both were unaware of the negotiations that led to the truce until after it was signed, and when Joan heard of it, she was despondent. On August 10, Joan plaintively confided to John of Orléans that, if it pleased God, she would prefer to go home to Domrémy and serve her parents in domestic and pastoral chores.

Charles meandered through the countryside of France toward Paris but set aside plans to attack the city once the truce had been signed. Towns along Charles' route readily submitted to the new king. On August 4, Bedford marched an army to the left bank of the Seine, and on August 15 the French and English skirmished but no major battle ensued. The English, sensing that the French would not engage in a decisive battle, retreated toward Paris the following day.

The Armagnacs continued to negotiate with Philip for his neutrality, but no agreement was finalized. On August 28, both sides agreed to a four-month truce that was to end on January 1, 1430. As part of the truce, Charles agreed to return cities to Philip that had acknowledged the king as their lord. Thirty-six days after departing from Reims, Charles completed the ninety-mile journey and reached Paris. English reinforcements had arrived by then and had substantially bolstered the city's defenses. Bedford named Philip as its governor, and the Duke of Burgundy, who had used the truce to temporize, now backed out of his promise.

Realizing Burgundian skullduggery, Charles reluctantly agreed to attack Paris on September 8—four months after the victory at Orléans—but by this time their chances of success were greatly diminished. The formidable walls were manned by English archers and Burgundians. Joan led from the front, exhorting the French and demanding that the defenders surrender to the king. Toward the end of the day, she was wounded in the thigh by a crossbow bolt and had to leave the field.

The attack failed, and Charles called off the assault on the following morning and ordered the army back to Saint-Denis. Joan and Alençon wanted to continue, but Charles commanded that they cease on September 10 and ordered the destruction of a bridge across the Seine that made a further attack impossible.[21] On September 12, having suffered casualties that numbered between one and two thousand, Charles acknowledged defeat and marched his army south toward the Loire.

Joan said a number of times during her public mission that she feared only treason or betrayal. On July 31, 1429, at Joan's request and in recognition of her contributions to crown and kingdom, Charles granted immunity from taxation to the citizens of Domrémy and Greux. On May 23, 1430, almost ten months from the bestowal of this favor, Joan was captured by Burgundians outside the walls of Compiègne and later sold to the English. No record survives that Charles did anything to procure her release.

---

[21] The bridge had been built earlier by Alençon.

19

The Sands of Time
Life at Court to Capture

Charles could not financially afford to provision an army large enough to take Paris for long. Those men-at-arms who did not depart on their own in September, hungry and unpaid, were disbanded in October. The towns that pledged allegiance to Charles on the march through northern France were left unprotected after the retreat and were once again absorbed by the English and Burgundians as more English reinforcements arrived from across the Channel.

Joan's wound needed time to heal, so she was sent to Bourges to rest for three weeks under the protection of the lord of Albret. Her hosts later gave testimony to her genuine piety, humility, and chastity. She may have thought again of going home to Domrémy when she understood that Charles had little inclination to fight and she probably would have left with his grateful blessing. Her friendship with Alençon had grown and their mutual collaboration stood in opposition to Charles' policy of patient negotiation. Whatever she thought, Joan opted to remain at court.

It was advantageous and even necessary for medieval kings and queens to have numerous castles and other lodgings to house their courts. Sanitation and hygiene were enduring concerns with so large a gathering in one place and a steady stream of visitors required for the functioning of a royal government. It was inevitable that refuse would accrue and the odor become so unpleasant, even intolerable, that a change of venue would become necessary to preserve royal dignity. Once the court had moved along its circuit to its next destination, a group of royal servants would sweep out and clean the vacant castle or stronghold of its filth and debris and ready it for the monarch's return.

Few peasants during the Middle Ages would have gained access to a royal court. Charles and his advisors, for example, deliberated for a few days before allowing Joan an audience even though they were in great distress, being pressed so vigorously by the English and Burgundians, and even though Joan had gained some local fame as la Pucelle who would save France. Fewer still were the peasants who resided in and traveled with a royal court. Most peasants would have been elated to have accomplished what Joan achieved and to have attained the status of a living legend, yet even the Act of Ennoblement in December 1429 did not seem to satisfy her. There would be no satisfaction or rest for Joan until she had accomplished the mission entrusted to her by her voices.

Joan was entirely discontent with court life, probably more so because Charles kept a lavish court. Her single-minded focus was to defeat the English and Burgundians or force surrender, but the king, following the advice of his counselors, forbade her to join Alençon for fear they would begin a military campaign and ruin Charles' diplomatic efforts with the Duke of Burgundy. This probably irked her since she admitted at her trial that she and most of the villagers of Domrémy loathed the Burgundians even more than they detested the English, no doubt because the marauders who raided them were mostly Burgundian.

Joan was valuable to Charles and had done him much good, but in most respects, they were ill-suited for one another. Charles was raised in a royal court, Joan in a peasant village. Charles was possessed of refined sensibilities and indulged himself in the pleasures of courtly life. Joan was abstemious and conditioned to the coarse manners and the pastoral life of peasant stock. Charles was cautious, suspicious, an administrator by nature, not a great military commander, preferring diplomacy to combat. Joan was courageous, resolute, loyal, strong-willed, a warrior and natural leader on the battlefield, even if she was untrained in war. When Joan was captured in 1430, Charles did the easiest thing he could do—nothing. She repaid his disloyalty by defending him before their enemies, proclaiming him to be a good Christian. In upbringing, class, temperament, and personal conduct, Charles and Joan were ill-matched from the start.

Joan did not fit well with his advisors either, and it was clear that she needed to be occupied and her talents put to good use. Perrinet Gressart was a French marauder captain working for the Anglo-Burgundian party. His wealth and power were growing, and he occupied a number of strongholds in central France as an agent for the English who paid him well. There was little risk involved in sending Joan with a group of soldiers to attack his fortifications, as it would not interfere with Charles' diplomatic efforts with Philip, so Joan was assigned the task of destroying Gressart's power base. This was not the mission she received from her voices, but she accepted the assignment anyway, probably to show loyalty to her king and to inflict justice on a band of marauders.

The stunning success she enjoyed up to the crowning at Reims was in short supply on this campaign. She managed to take Saint-Pierre-le-Moûtier by direct assault with only a few men in early November, but when the royal army laid siege to La Charité where Gressart was staying in mid-November, the winter weather, lack of supplies, and lack of support from Charles and his counselors forced Joan to lift the siege a month later. The failed siege not only caused her great displeasure, but her reputation at court and among the soldiers declined. She rejoined Charles' court, and in late December the king ennobled her and her family.

The new year of 1430 brought an end to the four-month truce signed on August 28 between Charles and Philip. The *esprit de corps* infused into the royal army by Joan's arrival and victories seeped away in the wake of the unpopular truce and no permanent peace had been established. Charles finally admitted in March 1430 to Philip's subterfuge.

To make matters worse, the English sent reinforcements and supplies to Normandy, and Philip was preparing to take by force the cities promised to him by Charles but which had not yet yielded. Reims was threatened as was Compiègne. In mid-April, Joan's voices told her that she would be captured before Saint John's Day on June 24.

The English and Burgundians initiated a new offensive that caught the Armagnac camp flat-footed. The king was still negotiating with Philip, and without informing him, Joan and a group of volunteers departed at the end of March. At Lagny she was given a dead baby, and as she cradled it the baby drew breath. It was immediately baptized and died shortly afterward, and Joan was credited with a miracle to public acclaim. She also captured Franquet of Arras, a mercenary loyal to the Anglo-Burgundians. She attempted to trade him for a captured comrade, Jacquet Guillaume, but when she learned that he had been executed, she handed Franquet over to local law officials who tried and executed him as a criminal. Later she and her army were rebuffed at Soissons, which professed loyalty to Burgundy, and many of her troops were disbanded for lack of food.

With her remaining soldiers she marched to Compiègne to prevent it from falling into Burgundian hands. On May 23, Joan and her companions sallied out from inside the city and attacked a small Burgundian outpost at Margny. After some initial success, the attack was repelled and many of her soldiers fled in retreat. Joan attempted to rally them but fell behind, and the city gate was closed before she could get inside. Surrounded by Burgundian troops and pulled from her horse by an English archer who threw her to the ground, and with no other choice but to surrender, she handed herself over to Lionel of Wandomme. Her squire, John of Aulon, and her brother Pierre were also captured. She was quickly brought to Margny and held under guard, and it was reported by a contemporary chronicler that the English and Burgundians were more joyous at Joan's capture than if they had captured five hundred Armagnac soldiers. Philip, attracted by this great novelty, came quickly to see her.

Their conversation was not recorded.

20

Desert Experience
Imprisonment

Lionel of Wandomme was in the service of John of Luxembourg, lord of Beaurevoir, and surrendered Joan to him shortly after her capture. Luxembourg was pro-Burgundian and in the pay of the English. He was the Duke of Burgundy's main representative in the negotiations that were held with Charles VII's counselors and took part in Philip's duplicitousness. He was also a well-seasoned military officer who had on numerous occasions despoiled lands loyal to Charles. After receiving Joan as a prisoner, he lifted the siege of the well-defended and well-provisioned Compiègne and moved Joan to his castle at Beaulieu.

Joan was an invaluable war prize and the English wanted her dearly. They believed she was a witch who had worked magical powers on them in battle, and they feared her for political reasons since she had become a symbol of French nationalism that could galvanize public sentiment on Charles' behalf. Luxembourg was not English, however, and was not obliged to hand her over to the English. According to custom, he had the right to exchange her for one or more other prisoners, ransom her to the highest bidder, or keep her in custody.

Joan attempted an escape from Beaulieu and was moved to Beaurevoir where she was treated humanely by Luxembourg's elderly aunt, Joan of Luxembourg, and his wife, Joan of Béthune. At her trial she testified that Joan of Luxembourg asked her nephew not to turn her over to the English, but the elder matron died in Avignon in September. In any case, John of Luxembourg was bound to Philip of Burgundy by an oath of fealty and therefore not entirely at liberty to do with Joan what pleased him or the ladies of his household.

During the months she was in the custody of Luxembourg, the English pressed the Burgundians to sell her to them and not to return her for ransom to the Armagnacs. The University of Paris, staunchly in the Anglo-Burgundian camp, sent a letter in late May requesting that Joan be handed over to the Church for an ecclesial trial. Pierre Cauchon took an active part in pressuring the Burgundians and visited Joan twice in prison. Cauchon was the former rector of the University of Paris and the current Bishop of Beauvais. He was also the former Bishop of Reims but abandoned the city and lost the bishopric when Reims pledged obedience to Charles at the time of his coronation. Cauchon had the reputation of being intelligent but severe, and wanted to bring Joan to a trial at which he presided.

There is no extant record of an offer from Charles or the Armagnacs to ransom Joan, yet it took months to finalize her sale to the English. One wonders why Luxembourg and the Burgundians hesitated. Perhaps it took time to negotiate the final price or gather the coinage, or perhaps they expected that Charles would eventually outbid the English. The king had financial difficulties, however, and perhaps for reasons of his own, he allowed Joan to be sold for 10,000 francs. The money was raised from taxes levied in Normandy.

Joan became highly distraught when she learned she had been sold to the English and further distressed when she heard that the citizens of Compiègne were to be massacred after a successful siege. She attempted to escape by jumping seventy feet from a tower into a dry moat and later testified that she preferred to die rather than to be turned over to the English and to see the people of Compiègne destroyed, but she denied any intent to commit suicide. Joan was injured from the fall, but in another remarkable display of her extraordinary physical abilities, she recovered quickly. She admitted at her trial that she was wrong to have jumped and that she did so against the counsel of her voices, who admonished her to confess her sin and be assured that the people of Compiègne would receive help from God. The siege was relieved on October 24.

Joan was heavily guarded as they transported her to Rouen, where she arrived on December 23. Many in Europe were astonished that she had fallen into English hands, and there was widespread belief that she would be rescued by God and freed. The English were wary of her and put her in chains. The normal procedure for one tried in an ecclesial court was to confine the prisoner in a Church prison that would have been far more comfortable than the abominable accommodations the English had arranged for Joan. There she would have been attended to by priests and women religious. But Cauchon and the English would not allow her this luxury. Joan was confined to a dark cell in a castle tower at the fortress of Bouvreuil and guarded by hardened soldiers—men "of the lowest rank"—three of whom slept in her cell at night while two remained by the door. She was always kept in leg irons, slept chained to her bed, and suffered the constant anxiety of possible rape. The guards cruelly tormented her with the loss of her virginity on many occasions in order to increase her mental anguish.

21

Capstone Experience
Interrogation and Trial
The Great Game

To the English Joan was a dangerous military adversary, and they kept her as a prisoner of war. A martyred Joan would be more dangerous to them than a living Joan, however, so they sought to discredit her as a heretic, blasphemer, or witch before putting her to death—an outcome that was never in question. Any disgrace that could be attributed to Joan would also taint Charles' reputation and challenge his legitimacy as king.

To Pierre Cauchon and the faculty at the University of Paris, Joan was a dangerous political opponent who they would not confine in an ecclesial prison for fear she might escape. She was a vigorous supporter of the king from whom they were estranged, and aligned with the Armagnacs whom they opposed. In their efforts to convict her of charges they could not substantiate, they were serving their own political and personal interests and those of the Anglo-Burgundian party and not those of the true Church.

But the matter in historical terms was a more complicated affair. The Church had suffered considerable loss of prestige from its impotence during the outbreak of the plague and the scandal of the Avignon Papacy and Western Schism. This crisis of authority was further complicated by the appearance of fourteenth-century reformers. The scholar John Wycliffe (d. 1384) translated the Bible into English and published it in 1382. A vernacular version of the Bible meant that any literate person could study and interpret Scripture independent of the authority of the Church. Wycliffe's ideas were later adopted by John Hus, who was burned as a heretic in 1415. This caused a rebellion in Bohemia among his followers that resulted in a series of civil wars lasting from 1419 until 1434. Church leaders were also disquieted by new spiritual movements that emphasized personal inspiration, private revelation, excessive veneration of the saints, and individual conscience. Moreover, the disenchantment of the masses on the secular plane that exploded in the Jacquerie in France and the Peasants' Revolt in England threatened not only civil authority but ecclesial as well.

The Church at the time of Joan's capture was struggling to emerge from a prolonged crisis of credibility, and its leaders were exerting power to regain lost respect. In the eyes of Cauchon and his ecclesial allies, Joan and her voices were an embodiment of the threat of religious populism to ecclesial authority, a threat they hoped to discredit and stamp out. Cauchon boasted they would conduct a "beautiful trial," but he must have been unpleasantly surprised at how events actually unfolded.

Joan was subject to another examination of her virginity before Anne of Burgundy, Duchess of Bedford, which she again passed. This was a blow to Cauchon and the English, as was the failure of the inquest into her life at Domrémy to find any fault or blame with which to discredit her.[22] Having ascertained that she was in truth a virgin and finding no evidence of heresy or witchcraft, the judges were unable to bring formal charges against her. Jean Lemaître, a Dominican friar and the vice-inquisitor, would have been the highest-ranking Church official at the trial, but he refused to participate on the grounds that it was against his conscience. The proceedings had not begun well for the judges, but they hoped to find a pretext for convicting her during her interrogation. Bedford and the English were demanding it.

Her trial began on January 9. There was never any doubt as to what the final verdict would be, and Joan probably knew this even if she never lost hope that some miraculous event would save her. Her life journey had now led her to walk in the footsteps of the Lord of History, who 1,400 years earlier was also handed over to the will of an implacable enemy, who also endured a sham trial and suffered a public, violent, and unjust death. In the end, the Annases and Caiaphases of her day and His could only rely on a misinterpretation of their words and groundless accusations, since no credible evidence was ever brought forth to convict either of them.

---

[22] Cauchon showed great displeasure with the results of the inquest at Domrémy.

The first session was held on Ash Wednesday, February 21. Before the actual interrogation began, Joan asked to attend Mass, but was refused on the grounds of the seriousness of the accusations against her. Cauchon opened the session by requiring Joan to swear with her hand on the Gospels that she would speak the truth regarding all that would be asked of her. She refused, saying that she did not know what would be asked of her and that she was told by her voices not to reveal certain secrets. The matter was concluded when a compromise was reached in which Joan swore to tell the truth about her religious beliefs but not everything regarding her private revelations.

She was then asked to state her name and give a brief account of her family background and hometown. Cauchon directed her to recite the Our Father, and Joan said she would do so only if he heard her confession. This put Cauchon in an awkward position. If he declined to hear her confession, he would be neglecting a ministerial responsibility. If he consented, he would be held under the sacramental seal and obliged not to reveal what she had said. This first session was a precursor of what was to come—a duel of intellect and will between Joan, who was deprived of a lawyer, and Cauchon and his allies, who were highly trained theologians and members of the faculty of the University of Paris. Joan held her ground so well, however, that Cauchon later moved the trial from the public hall in the castle to the privacy of her cell.

Among the forty or so prelates and doctors of theology were scribes who recorded the proceedings. One of these was

Guillaume Manchon, who later reported that he was urged to misrepresent Joan's words. He also testified that one notary was recording an unofficial copy. Manchon's complaints to Cauchon about these irregularities resulted only in an angry reprimand.

The reluctant Dominican Jean Lemaître finally came to Rouen to attend the second session on February 22 after Cauchon had written letters to his religious superior, but he was only an intermittent participant for the remainder of the trial and was largely absent. Lemaître was probably annoyed by the tactics employed by Joan's interrogators. Since there was no evidence of guilt and no crime with which to formally charge her, the prelates attempted to confuse Joan and wear her down by asking multiple questions at the same time, sometimes by more than one interrogator. She was frequently interrupted, causing her much vexation. Another tactic was to ask her the same question at different sessions and then compare her answers, looking for some inconsistency.

But Joan was equal to the task. She bore the hardships of imprisonment by the English with great fortitude and maintained remarkable composure before her ecclesial judges. She was always in shackles, chained at night to a heavy wooden block, and always guarded by Englishmen "of the lowest rank." Her voices told her to answer boldly and she answered so astutely that the notaries were instructed to begin recording her answers in the third person rather than the first person to lessen the impact of her statements. Several of those present credited Joan with an outstanding memory and sagacity that was far beyond her years and level of education.

Finding no evidence of heresy, blasphemy, or witchcraft, her judges questioned her at length about her wearing of men's clothing. She testified that she strove to obey the will of God in all things and that the style of her clothes was an unimportant matter. The Armagnacs had accepted Joan's male attire as a practical accommodation since she lived among men and often rode a horse. It also made religious sense since she was commanded by her voices to preserve her virginity, and trousers were far more effective at deterring rape than a dress. The inquisitors periodically returned to this topic as part of their strategy to confuse and tire her.

Joan defended herself on this and all other points so well that the trial was becoming a public embarrassment to Cauchon and his allies, and an exhibition of Joan's courage and intelligence pitted against the bias and vehemence of her enemies. This promoted sympathy for Joan among those assessors who were not allied with Cauchon. A number of them criticized the heavy-handedness of the Bishop of Beauvais, and some of them quietly departed from Rouen when it became apparent that Cauchon was willing to resort to violence. Switching tactics, Cauchon and three other selected judges began visiting Joan in her cell in order to conduct the interrogation privately—one of many irregularities that were brought forth during her trial of rehabilitation.

Private interrogations in Joan's cell continued almost daily from March 10 until March 17, but despite intense questioning by multiple professors from the University of Paris and the threat of torture, no evidence of guilt could be found in her. This ended the preliminary phase of Joan's canonical trial in which the accused was questioned and permitted an opportunity to recant before the ordinary trial began. Throughout this ordeal, Joan was comforted almost daily by her voices who said she would be delivered from her sufferings and that she should accept martyrdom with serenity. She supposed that by martyrdom her voices meant the hardships of her trial and imprisonment, and she continued to hope that her life might be spared by some calamity that would set her free. But her voices had something else in mind.

The next phase of the trial began on March 26. During the interim period since March 17, a list of seventy formal charges was put in writing and read to Joan on March 27 and 28. Joan's words were misrepresented and many of the articles were based on falsified records. Some of the articles were mere fabrication. Joan was required to respond to each charge after it was read but she remained steadfast in the answers she had previously given. She refused to deny the authenticity of her voices and the divine origin of her mission. Frustrated and without actual evidence, Cauchon knew the only way he could convict her was to force her to admit guilt. He demanded that she submit to his authority and that of the other prelates gathered at Rouen as representative of the Church's authority on earth.

Joan was interrogated privately again on March 31. Growing more desperate and with the English pressing for a conviction, her interrogators again demanded that she submit to their authority and admit guilt. She had previously responded to this demand during the preliminary phase that she would submit to the pope if she were brought to see him, but this was denied her. She also defended herself by insisting that her first responsibility was to obey the will of God, which she always strove to do, and to obey the counsel of her voices since they represented to her God's will. Joan's reluctance to submit to the will of Cauchon and the other judges by admitting guilt was interpreted as an offense against the authority of the Church.

Between April 2 and April 7, the seventy articles drawn up against Joan were condensed to twelve and submitted to the assessors at Rouen and theologians at the University of Paris. Joan fell ill after eating fish sent to her from Cauchon's table. She believed she had been poisoned and stated this to her doctors. The Bishop of Beauvais may have resorted to additional pernicious means to weaken Joan, as he was under great pressure from the English to secure a conviction. They did not wish her to die in prison, however. Cauchon visited her again on April 18 to demand her submission to the judges' authority.

The theologians at the University of Paris unanimously agreed on Joan's guilt, but not all of the assessors agreed to convict her without further attempts to convince her to submit to the authority of the Church. This kept Cauchon in a difficult position.

Once again demonstrating her astonishing physical and mental stamina, Joan recovered from her illness. On May 10, she was threatened with torture before two executioners, Maugier Leparmentier and his assistant. She responded that even if they pulled her limb from limb, she would not answer any more questions or change any of her answers. Leparmentier was present at her execution on May 30 and testified to Joan's heroism and the pity expressed by many of the bystanders, including some of the English.

On May 24, Cauchon arranged to have Joan brought to the cemetery at the Abbey of Saint-Ouen where platforms were built. On one platform stood Church dignitaries, abbots from local monasteries, and her judges. Joan was escorted onto a separate platform opposite the dignitaries and listened to a sermon preached by Guillaume Érard full of recriminations denouncing her alleged crimes. At one point he denounced Charles VII, and Joan interrupted to defend the king but was told to be quiet. When Érard concluded, Joan again appealed to God and the pope.

Eyewitness testimonies differ at this point. What is clear is that a document was presented to her to sign that contained an abjuration. One eyewitness, Aimond of Macy, said that Laurence Calot, secretary to the King of England, presented Joan with the document and held her hand as she signed with a cross. Jean Massieu, who was on the platform with her, gave a different account. He testified that she did not understand the document and asked to have it explained to her by some of the clerics. Érard merely told her to sign it in submission to the Church. The document, according to Jean Massieu, was about eight lines long and stipulated among other promises that Joan would no longer wear men's clothing, cut her hair short, and never again take up arms against the English. Massieu recounted that the document entered into the official record, however, contained forty-seven lines in which she admitted her voices were evil spirits and that she was guilty of the religious crimes with which she was charged.

It is also uncertain how Joan expected to be treated once she signed the abjuration. It is probable that she thought she would spend a few years in a Church prison and then be allowed to go home to Domrémy as was the custom for heretics who repented. She would also be allowed to hear Mass and receive the sacraments during her imprisonment. Once she signed the document, however, she learned she would be kept in an English prison under English guard for the remainder of her life, a fate she dreaded.

The English were incensed at Cauchon and the other Church officials. They had paid handsomely for Joan when they purchased her from the Burgundians and wanted to execute her. Some of the English nobles drew swords against the churchmen, but one of the clerics assured the English that Joan would not escape the end the English desired for her.

Cauchon ordered Joan to be taken back to her cell. She was given a dress to wear and had her head shaved as was customary for penitent heretics. Three days later, Joan was again wearing men's clothes. We are not certain of the events of those three days, but it seems that Joan was harassed by the English guards and her virginity threatened. Massieu testified that the English took her dress away one night and left her men's clothes. Having no other option, Joan began wearing them on May 27.

Whatever occurred, Cauchon, Jean Lemaître, and a number of other judges came to visit her the next morning. She told them she had resumed wearing men's clothes of her own volition since she was living among men and because she did not receive what was promised, namely, that she was confined in an English prison and not in a Church prison, that she was kept in fetters, and that she was not allowed to receive Communion. She said she would return to women's clothes only if the promises were kept. When questioned about her voices, she said they had visited her again and told her that she was wrong to have signed the abjuration. She reiterated that at no time did she ever intend to renounce her voices and added that it was the fear of being burned alive that weakened her resolve. It was clear to the judges that Joan had recovered her confident defiance and that she dreaded spending the rest of her life in an English prison.

Cauchon now had the pretext he needed to convict her as a relapsed heretic. On May 30, she was visited in prison by two Dominicans. Martin Ladvenu heard her confession and informed her that she would be handed over to the English for execution and burned at the stake that day. Joan began to weep and wail aloud, pulling her hair and protesting to God that she had been treated with extreme injustice. She particularly lamented the harshness and violence of the English guards and bitterly reproached Cauchon on his next visit as the reason for her mortal misfortune.

It was reported later by Jean Massieu that Joan asked Ladvenu after her confession if she could receive the Eucharist. Ladvenu was unsure and sent a messenger to Cauchon to ask for permission. In one of the most surprising events of this trial, Cauchon told the messenger to allow her to receive the Eucharist and to give her anything else she wanted. To allow an excommunicated and relapsed heretic to receive Communion would have been sacrilegious, and that Cauchon permitted it puts into question whether or not he truly believed that Joan was in a state of mortal sin and guilty of the crimes with which she was convicted.

22

Deus ex Machina
Joan's Hero-Moment
Virgin, Hero, Martyr, Saint

The platforms were again erected the next day, this time at the Old Marketplace where Joan would spend her final, painful moments. She was ushered from her prison cell by English guards and a few sympathetic assessors onto a cart that was waiting outside and then taken through the streets of Rouen to the place of execution. Onlookers jeered and moaned at the fate of the unfortunate, and a large crowd gathered to hear Nicolas Midy preach a final sermon denouncing Joan. According to Jean Massieu, there were eight hundred armed English soldiers on hand to ensure there would be no rescue or escape.

Throughout the entire spectacle, Joan prayed aloud to her voices and the God she trusted would save her. When Midy had finished his sermon, Cauchon stepped forward to pronounce the verdict. After listing her alleged offenses and the means the Church had used to bring her to repentance, he pronounced the ecclesial penalty of excommunication and formally handed her over to the English for execution. It was noted later at Joan's trial of rehabilitation that Cauchon never actually obtained a sentence in a secular court before handing her over to be executed, which was a serious omission as the Church did not have the authority to condemn people to death.

In a moment the guards jostled her onto the scaffold and demanded the executioner, Geoffrey Thérage, perform his duty. As Joan was being chained to the stake, she asked for a cross and an Englishman standing nearby made one from two sticks and handed it to her. She kissed it devoutly while uttering loud prayers and put it in her bosom. Friar Isambart de La Pierre left the scene for a nearby church and returned carrying a cross, which she asked to have held high so she could see it as she burned. Massieu was on the scaffold with her and provided her with sympathy and comfort. He was finally confronted by an English captain who asked if the friar intended to keep them there "until dinnertime."

The all-too-eager English guards hastened the clerics off the scaffold and pressed Thérage to consummate the bishop's decree and conclude the gruesome matter. He hesitated in the final instant before approaching but nonetheless complied, dolefully conceding to a perceived inevitability of the moment just as Pilate had 1,400 years earlier. The firewood surrounding Joan was lit and flames cracked the kindling as smoke wafted through and above the crowd. The wood had been set farther back from the stake so as to make her death more painful, a final testament to the vindictiveness of her enemies. The heat became more intense and

Joan's plaintive voice could still be heard, clear and strong, her loud lamentations accompanying the smoke as it rose to heaven like incense from an ancient Hebrew holocaust.

"JESUS! . . ."

The flames rose quickly above the pyre.

"JESUS! . . ."

Many of the English guard fell silent, not as confident as they once were of the rightness of their cause.

"JESUS! . . ."

The banter of the crowd lessened as the people of Rouen strained to hear her dying words.

"JESUS! . . ."

The flames engulfed the unfortunate as the crackle rose to an infernal din. Bedford wondered for a moment how such an execution would promote English interests. Cauchon suppressed an interior reproach that threatened to break through his implacable determination.

"JESUS! . . ."

Many of the bystanders were moved to pity and some to tears. Even among the English guard, hardened hearts were softened as they sometimes are when the life of one of our own, born of a human mother, is about to be extinguished.

"JESUS! . . ."

Before her end, Thérage knew. He did not convict this woman of any crime or torture her for a meaningless confession. He was only doing his duty, but he knew they were killing a saint.

"JESUS! . . ."

. . . Said the voice one last time, her figure hardly discernible amidst the devouring inferno.

At last, her head dropped, and she spoke no more.

~

The crackle of the flames continued. Silence otherwise prevailed.

The deed was done. Her enemies had gotten their wish. A sense of closure pervaded the scene but there was little sense of accomplishment among those who once believed she was their enemy. Regret and sorrow, felt formerly only in seed if at all, now sprang into full blossom, and even among the English guard there were men whose hearts were changed forever.

The deed had been done in the openness of a public square for all of heaven to see—as if its candid nature made it morally justifiable.

Neither witch, nor blasphemer, nor whore. Bedford wondered what would come of this now.

~

Her remains were burned three times. When the flames finally died down, the English gathered her ashes and cast them into the Seine. There would be no memorial, no gravesite, no tombstone, no final testament to this young heroine from Domrémy except that which history and the Church finally accorded her.

23

Victory and Vindication
The Hundred Years' War (1431 to 1453)

After Joan's death and believing they had dispatched a dangerous foe, the English renewed their campaign against Charles and the Armagnacs by besieging Louviers, which surrendered on October 28, 1431. Charles' brother-in-law, King René of Anjou, was taken prisoner at the Battle of Bulgnéville, and a royal army was defeated near Beauvais and Champagne. Henry VI, the nine-year-old King of England, was brought to France to be anointed King of France at Notre Dame in Paris on Sunday, December 16. Absent was the holy vial kept at Saint-Rémy Abbey in Reims.

On February 20, 1432, John of Orléans retook Chartres, and later that year the Duke of Bedford was forced to lift the siege of Lagny. An assassination attempt on La Trémoïlle at Chinon failed because he was so overweight that the sword only caused a superficial wound. He was imprisoned for a short time and expelled from Charles' court. This signaled a change in the way Charles and his advisors would conduct their internal affairs.

France's citizenry desired greater military action against the English, and La Trémoïlle would have to be replaced.

Diplomatic efforts nevertheless continued between Charles and the Burgundians. A breakthrough came when Bedford's wife, who was also the Duke of Burgundy's sister, died in 1432. A strong tie between Bedford and Burgundy had now been dissolved, and Philip's sympathy for the English cause waned. Peace talks between the French and Burgundians were held at Nevers in January 1435 but concluded without a treaty. Another round of talks that included the English was held at Arras in August, although the English delegates departed after six weeks, refusing to negotiate over Normandy or the kingship of France. Bedford died at Rouen on September 12, which left a power vacuum as he was Henry VI's regent in France. He was replaced by Louis of Luxembourg, who did not have the skills and tact of his predecessor and alienated himself from the citizenry of Paris.

Bedford's death effectively ended the Anglo-Burgundian alliance as it removed an important obstacle to reconciliation between Charles and Philip. The Treaty of Arras was signed on September 21, and Philip acknowledged Charles as the rightful King of France. In return, Charles granted Philip additional lands and promised to have his representative apologize on his knees before Philip for the murder of John the Fearless. He also promised to build a monument in John's name.

The civil war was at long last over, and the Burgundians abandoned the English cause. Ironically, Charles' mother, Isabeau of Bavaria, who supported the Treaty of Troyes and the disinheritance of Charles to the throne of France, died on September 24.

The English derided the Treaty of Arras as a betrayal by Philip of Henry. The tide of war turned more fully against the English as popular uprisings in northern France forced them to abandon their remaining strongholds. In February 1436, French forces under the Constable Arthur of Richemont, who had replaced La Trémoïlle in Charles' court, besieged Paris. He was aided by John of Orléans and the Burgundian Villiers de l'Isle Adam. On April 17, 1436, Richemont entered the city with the help of Paris' citizenry. After a brief period of negotiation, the English garrison was permitted to depart safely but did so to a chorus of boos and jeers. In 1437, Charles entered Paris in triumph, thus fulfilling Joan's prediction in 1429 at Poitiers that Paris would once again return its allegiance to Charles within seven years.

Another of Joan's predictions would be fulfilled in 1440 when Charles, Duke of Orléans, returned to France after twenty-five years in modestly comfortable English captivity. The year 1440 also saw a conspiracy against Charles VII, known as the Praguerie, by disaffected members of the nobility that included his former ally, the Duke of Alençon, and the Dukes of Bourbon and Brittany, who were jealous of Richemont's power. Also implicated was the Duke of Burgundy and Charles' son, Louis the dauphin, who sought real power that Charles was unwilling to give. For the remainder of the king's life, Charles would have a tumultuous relationship with his ambitious son, and in 1446 the king banished his heir to the Dauphiny. Charles later demanded that Louis return to court, but Louis refused and eventually took refuge with Philip in 1456.

Fighting between the French and English continued, although some of the English nobility, including the Dukes of Beaufort and Suffolk, advocated for peace. Suffolk managed to arrange the Truce of Tours in 1444, which lasted two years and stipulated that the French would gain control of the county of Le Maine and Henry VI would receive as a bride Margaret of Anjou, daughter of René of Anjou and Charles' sixteen-year-old niece. They were married in February 1445 and she was crowned queen in May. Margaret was headstrong and thoroughly French, and did not support the English king's claim to the throne of France. Henry, conversely, had a feeble mind and weak constitution, and she was able to gain some level of control over him. The people of England despised her as their queen.

Le Maine was surrendered to the French in 1448 and the truce was renewed for another two years until 1450. In 1449, the English raided the border fortress of Fougéres, which gave Charles a pretext for a campaign in Normandy. The king had reformed the French army over the years, making it the first fully paid standing army in Europe. His reforms also included the development of artillery and the training of artillery officers. The French campaign in Normandy began in July 1449, and Charles entered its capital, Rouen, in November after its citizenry revolted against the English. The English garrison was permitted safe passage out of the city, but Talbot, their commander, was required to remain a prisoner.

On March 15, 1450, Thomas Kyriell landed at Cherbourg with four thousand English troops and marched to relieve the French siege of Bayeux. He was intercepted by the Count of Clermont near the village of Formigny. The French refused to charge as they had at Crécy, Poitiers, and Agincourt, and instead employed their canonry. Richemont arrived toward the evening in support of Clermont, and the English reinforcements were destroyed. This made it impossible for the English to defend Normandy.

English kings had enjoyed possession of the powerful duchy of Normandy since 1066 when William the Conqueror won the English crown from Harold Godwinson at the Battle of Hastings. The Norman Conquest of England provided a perennial source of friction between the kings of England and France, and the year 1066 may be viewed as the origin of the Hundred Years' War. Almost four hundred years later this thorn was removed from the French king's side and Charles VII would be credited with victory in the Hundred Years' War. The fate of his counterpart, Henry VI of England, would be a much less happy one.

Once Charles gained control of Rouen, he called for his counselor, Guillaume Bouillé, to begin an investigation into Joan's trial and execution. Those participants who were still alive were summoned to testify beginning May 2, 1450. Among them were:

- Guillaume Manchon (notary)
- Pierre Miget (judge)
- Four Dominican friars: Isambart de La Pierre, Martin Ladvenu (who were with Joan on the scaffold), Guillaume Duval, and Jean Toutmouillé
- Jean Massieu (who ushered Joan from her cell to the courtroom before each hearing)
- Jean Beaupére (a supporter of Cauchon).

Those unable to attend the inquest included three of Joan's most implacable enemies:

- Pierre Cauchon (d. 1442)
- Jean d'Estivet (d. 1438)
- Nicolas Midy (d. 1442).

The proceedings culminated in a petition to the Holy See for a trial of rehabilitation. On November 7, 1455, in a public ceremony arranged by Charles and his advisors and conducted at Notre Dame Cathedral in Paris, Isabelle Romée, Joan's aged mother, asked three representatives of the pope for a trial of rehabilitation. The trial was moved to the Great Hall at Rouen and concluded on July 7, 1456, with a declaration of nullity.

Between the initial investigation and final verdict, the French continued to pressure English holdings in France. In 1453, Charles sent French troops into Guyenne and Gascony to finally drive the English from France. The Battle of Castillon was fought on July 17, which was the first time field artillery was used extensively on the battlefield. It was the English turn to charge, and French cannon mowed them down by the dozen. Those who were not killed surrendered. The victory was decisive, and after three centuries under English occupation, the French had finally recovered Gascony and Guyenne.[23]

They did not know at the time, but Castillon marked the end of the Hundred Years' War. Only Calais remained in English hands. In another ironic twist of fate, England would soon descend into its own civil war, the Wars of the Roses, which lasted from 1455 to 1485.

---

[23] That same year, 1453, Constantinople fell to the Ottoman Turks.

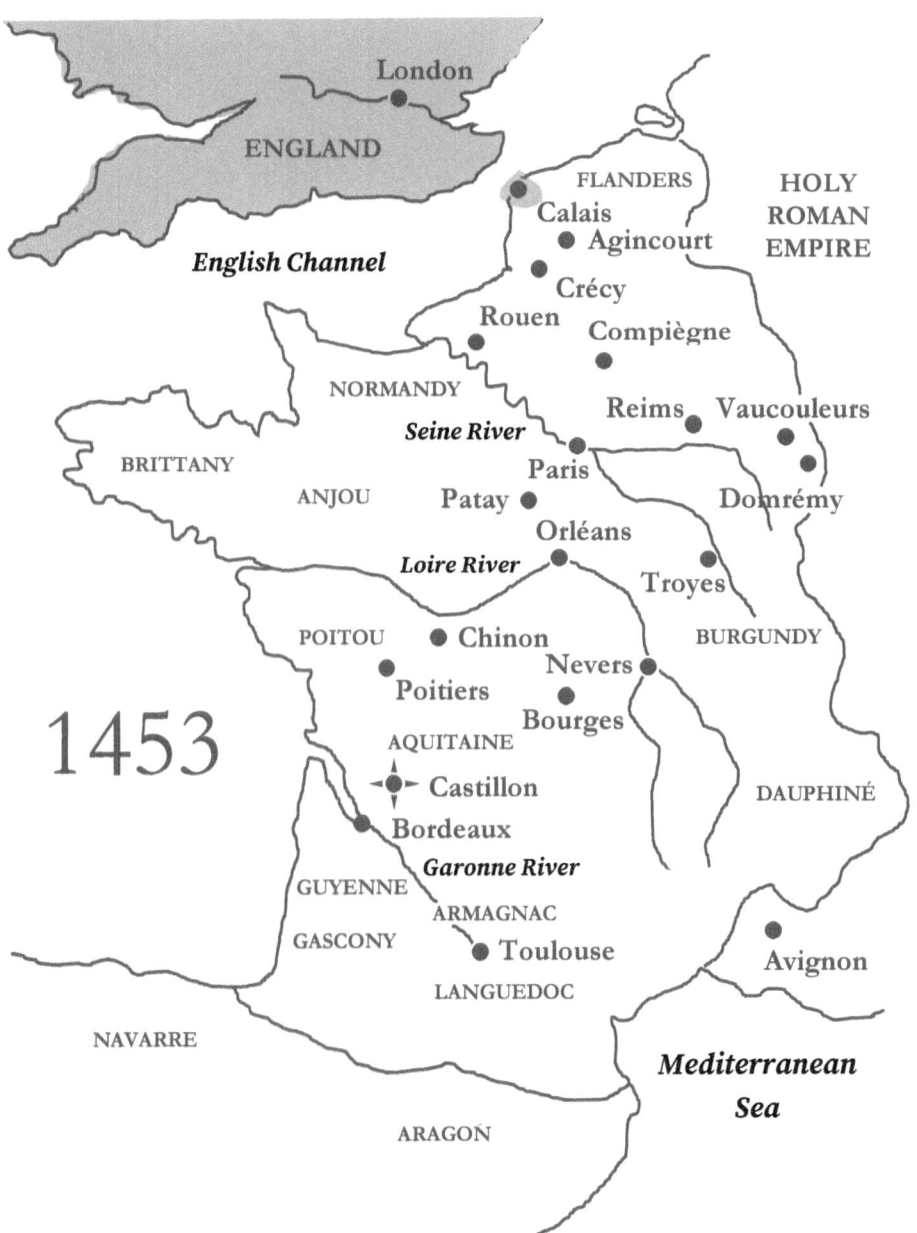

Conclusion

Historians rightly attempt to evaluate Joan's success as a military commander. Her accomplishments were due in large part to her dynamic personality, the inspiration and morale boost she provided to the troops, and her single-minded determination to obey her voices. Joan was on a mission in every sense, never leaving ambiguity as to what that mission was.

After her contribution at the Battle of Orléans, the results of her military endeavors were a mixed bag. Much of the credit for the final victory over the English was due to commanders like John of Orléans, Alençon, and La Hire. Having no training in the military sciences, Joan's repertoire of strategy and tactics was limited. If letters and verbal threats failed to induce compliance, her only alternative was relentless attack. With banner in hand, she was often in the midst of the troops or leading a charge. Diplomacy was never a part of Joan's calculus in warfare, which diverged sharply with Charles' policy with the Burgundians.

But the question remains: Would the French have won without her? It is probable they would not have. Most at the time believed the English were on the verge of victory during the siege of Orléans, but Joan's sudden and unexpected arrival breathed new hope into the demoralized royal army, and she played an indispensable part in lifting the siege and during the Loire Campaign. In her first battle at Saint-Loup, she arrived late on the battlefield after having been awoken from a nap by her voices. Her appearance had an immediate impact on the morale of the troops, and for the first time during the siege at Orléans, the French were able to dislodge the English from one of their fortifications. Confidence in her steadily grew until she reached her apex at Reims.

France had no one who could dispel the hopelessness that permeated the Armagnac camp until Joan appeared. She appealed to their religious convictions and sense of French identity in a way no one else could. She provided leadership in word and deed and instilled confidence in the dauphinist cause that God would bring victory. She alone among all maidens could assure she was from God and bring tangible results as proof. But she could not play the part of a military strategist—that assignment necessarily fell to others. Despite her overweening self-confidence at times, she was unsuited for this role.

When it came to her true mission and vocation, however, Joan was profoundly successful. It is remarkable that she was able to persuade Baudricourt at Vaucouleurs to provide her with an armed escort to Chinon, and then be admitted into the royal hall with nothing more than a letter of recommendation and her reputation as the maiden who would save France. She recognized Charles in a crowd without ever having seen him, and when he tested her further by pointing to another man standing nearby and identified him as the dauphin, she saw through his subterfuge. In less than a month she was awarded a place in the Armagnac army, even if it was not the command she thought she deserved. Victory at Orléans confirmed her authenticity and cemented her stature in the geopolitical events of her day. Her place in history was permanently secured when she convinced the dauphin to travel to Reims and was present at his coronation dressed in armor.

The mixed bag of military results that followed Orléans in no way diminishes the success of her true mission and vocation, but instead reveals it. Her capture began a train of events that ensured her story would forever be told in the pages of history and in eternity. Her canonization was her coronation—a final victory over the Sanhedrin that tried her and handed her over to death. Her voices had always assured her of deliverance, but she gave no sign she understood how grand it would be.

~

Joan was canonized on May 16, 1920, almost five hundred years after her martyrdom. On May 17, 1925—almost five years to the day—another female French saint who died young was also canonized. Their lives could hardly have been more different, even if they were marked by a number of ironic coincidences:

- Joan was a medieval peasant living in the early fifteenth century and in the shadow of the appalling fourteenth century. Thérèse Martin was a member of the nineteenth-century bourgeois class and lived a provincial life in a peaceful and prosperous Normandy.

- Joan was one of five children, none of whom entered religious life. Thérèse was one among five surviving children (four died in infancy), all of whom entered religious life.

- It is believed that Joan was born on January 6 (Epiphany). It is known that Thérèse was born on January 2. Thérèse was born in Alençon, and Joan became great friends and comrades with John II, Duke of Alençon, who she called her "fair duke."

- Thérèse was born in 1873 after the Franco-Prussian War and died in 1897 during the military buildup to World War I, but France was never at war during her lifetime. Joan lived her whole life in the shadow of war, and her mission necessitated that she participate in armed conflict.

- Joan showed no regret for having left her family and testified at her trial that she would do it again if God called her to it. Thérèse, on the other hand, was highly attached to her family. Her mother, Zelie Guerin, died when she was four and a half years old, and Thérèse experienced a nervous breakdown. She also became highly distressed when her sisters left home for the convent, and when Pauline departed, Thérèse seemed close to death. Later as a Carmelite sister, she was deeply grieved when her father, Louis Martin, was slowly dying in 1894.

153

- From the time of her mother's death until her early teens, Thérèse was highly sensitive, shy, and timid, and was frequently subject to fits of tears. Joan was also prone to outbursts of tears and showed remorse at the sight of dead soldiers, but she was not particularly sensitive or shy and regularly changed clothes in front of male soldiers.

- Joan was called by her voices to active military service and to the geopolitical events of her day. Thérèse was called to a convent and the life of a contemplative, cloistered nun.

- Thérèse was deferential to authority, often professed to be "weak" and "powerless," and she referred to herself as "the Little Flower." Joan was boastful, endowed with a warrior spirit, was dynamic and authoritative during her military service, and showed a lack of deference toward authority, even royal authority.

- Like many French citizens of her time, Thérèse looked to Joan as a symbol of French nationalism and was devoted to her as a saint. She wrote a play about Joan and played her part in a performance before her religious community. She also wrote several poems about Joan.

- No image survives of Joan, but her contemporaries made almost no mention of her beauty. It is apparent from Thérèse's pictures that she was attractive, and she was noted by her contemporaries for her beauty.

- Joan crowned a king. Thérèse met a pope.

- Joan was not literate, but her story was written in the transcripts of her two trials. Thérèse was asked by her religious superior, Mother Marie de Gonzague, to write a story of her life, which has since become a popular Catholic classic entitled *The Story of a Soul*. Both saints have had many books written about them.

- Joan was publicly martyred at age nineteen. Her dying moments were cruelly painful but relatively brief. Thérèse died at twenty-four in obscurity from tuberculosis. Her death was prolonged and painful because her religious superior believed that professed religious should suffer without painkilling medication, and she did not allow Thérèse to receive morphine. Her final agony lasted twelve hours.

- Joan became famous for her important contributions in the Hundred Years' War and was named a patron saint of France at the time of her canonization. Thérèse became famous and was named the thirty-third Doctor of the Church for her understanding of "spiritual childhood" and the doctrine of her "Little Way."

- Joan's mission, in her own words, was to:

    1. Drive out the English

    2. Bring the dauphin to Reims to be crowned king

    3. Free Charles, Duke of Orléans, from captivity in England

    4. Raise the siege of Orléans.

- At the end of her life, Thérèse said of her mission:

> I feel that my mission is soon to begin, to make others love God as I do, to teach others my "little way." I will spend my Heaven in doing good upon earth.[24]

Despite their many differences, Joan and Thérèse have much in common, namely they:

- Were united in their devotion to God's will and their supreme confidence in Providence

- Had mothers who were devout and provided them with religious instruction

- Were virgins

- Were called to a mission

- Had a hero-event and hero-moment: Joan in her public mission that culminated in her martyrdom, and Thérèse in her final illness that culminated in a slow and painful death

- Demonstrated heroic charity—the main qualification required of a candidate for sainthood (i.e., the love of God and neighbor to a heroic degree)

- Became well-loved and widely known saints.

---

[24] St. Thérèse of Lisieux, *The Story of a Soul: The Autobiography of St. Thérèse of Lisieux*, trans. Michael Day, (Charlotte, NC: TAN Books, 2010), 173–4.

The above comparison between Joan the Maiden and Thérèse of Lisieux illustrates the principle that hero-saints can be found in all walks of life, at all times, and in all places, from those who are lowly and obscure to those who become famous in history. As the story of our life is being written day by day, we should ask ourselves in the light of these hero-stories of the saints if we are on a hero-quest or a fool's quest:

- Are our priorities in life rightly ordered?

- Do we live a life of virtue and remain close to God in prayer?

- Are we answering God's call to the hero story he wants to write with our life?

- Where do we expect our life journey to end?

- What role does the Lord of History play in our life story?

It is a fundamental spiritual truth that we always get what we want when it comes to God, but does God always get what he wants when it comes to us? And we should ask ourselves in a quiet, reflective moment before God: Is there any better way to spend one's life than with the hope of becoming a saint?

> I must admit that when I read certain tales of chivalry, I did not always grasp the realities of life; in my enthusiasm I wanted to do all the patriotic things the heroines of France had done, especially Joan of Arc. It was at this time that I was given what I have always considered one of my life's greatest

graces. . . [God] taught me that the only glory which matters is the glory which lasts forever and that one does not have to perform shining deeds to win that. . . [T]hen it was revealed to me in my heart that my glory would lie in becoming a Saint, though this glory would be hidden on earth.[25]

—Saint Thérèse of Lisieux

---

[25] St. Thérèse of Lisieux, *Story of a Soul*, 40.

About the Author

Brother Emmanuel Labrise, O.S.B., received a B.S. from Saint Vincent College, an M.A. from Bowling Green State University, and an M.A. from Notre Dame Seminary. A contemplative monk with over twenty years' experience in monastic life, he spent six years as a member of the Order of Carthusians and has been a monk in the Order of Saint Benedict since 2009. Among other assignments, he has taught in a seminary college, worked in a seminary formation program, and given conferences at a retreat house. He is currently living the eremitical life in which his main activities are prayer, reading, reflection, and writing.

Books by Brother Emmanuel Labrise, O.S.B.
A Hero Is Chosen Series
Hero Stories of the Saints

Book One: *Reflections of an Uncommon Monk: Toward a*
Theology of Hero-Sainthood
Serves as an introduction to the series and its spiritual
and moral foundation

Book Two: *Mission of the Maiden: The Hero Story of Joan of Arc*

Part One: Historical Context
Fourteenth- and fifteenth-century medieval
Europe; High Middle Ages; Hundred Years'
War; history of France and England

Part Two: Mission of the Maiden
Joan's hero-saint story focusing on her public
mission (hero-event) from the time she left
Domrémy until her interrogation, trial, and
burning at the stake (hero-moment)

Book Three: *God's Good Servant and the King's: The Hero Story of*
Thomas More

Part One: Historical Context
Fifteenth- and sixteenth-century Renaissance
Europe; Reformation period; English and
Church history

Part Two: God's Good Servant and the King's
Thomas More's hero-saint story focusing on
his public dissent from King Henry VIII (hero-
event) until his execution (hero-moment)

Book Four: *King of Kings: The Hero Story of Jesus of Nazareth*

    Part One: Historical Context
                    Old and New Testament history; first-century
                    AD Roman occupation of Judea

    Part Two: King of Kings
                    Jesus of Nazareth's hero-saint story focusing
                    on his public mission (hero-event) from his
                    baptism in the Jordan by John the Baptist until
                    his crucifixion at Calvary (hero-moment)

Book Five: *Friar, Priest, and Martyr: The Hero Story of Maximilian Kolbe*

    Part One: Historical Context
                    Nineteenth- and twentieth-century Europe; the
                    rise of German nationalism; Nazism and World
                    War II

    Part Two: Friar, Priest, and Martyr
                    Maximilian's hero-saint story focusing on his
                    public mission as a priest (hero-event) until his
                    imprisonment and death at Auschwitz (hero-moment)

Book Six: *A Vocation Story Never Told: A Hero Story of Future Saints*
                    Short fiction novella that takes place in the late
                    twenty-second century and early twenty-third century

Book Seven: *Hero Bible Verses: Meditations of a Saint*
                    Inspiring Bible quotes from Genesis to Revelation

Notes and Personal Reflections:

Notes and Personal Reflections:

Notes and Personal Reflections: